Winning the Contractor Fight

ISBN: 978-1-7379191-0-0

Imprint: Independently Published

Cover design by: Mike Shortsleve
Cover layout by: Amber Castañeda

Edited by: Kathryn Tague

There are people in this world who make others stronger. Who bring out the best in us and prove time and again that they are in our corner. For me, this person is my Queen.

Lee, this book doesn't happen without your encouragement and kick in the ass.

You Make Me Feel Taller.

Deborah Ann Verdico... you gave me Life & taught me how to love unconditionally. I miss you, Mom. I'm proud to be your son.

Legal Disclaimer

Table of Contents

Winning the Contractor Fight

Tom Reber

Foreword #1

Tom is ahead of the curve.

10 years ago, I stepped off stage after presenting to an audience of 1,000 contractors. My topic was "how to get the bottom line you want."

Tom was one of the first to greet me. He said, "all that stuff you just shared was fantastic, but you missed the big point!"

I was thinking, "who the hell is this guy?". Tom said, "I'm a business coach and THE most important aspect of running a business is your mindset." I thought, "great, I'm not off stage for two minutes and this guy is going to try and sell me his services."

Little did I know that Tom was 100% correct.

Tom and I became great friends and started an online coaching business together. The Contractor Sales Academy. C.S.A.

I was blinded by the big picture because I thought that everyone thought like me when it came to running your business. I couldn't have been more wrong. Tom couldn't have been more right. We all carry the baggage of our past stored in the subconscious. This affects how we act in adulthood.

This book will teach you the mental skills you must have to properly run your business. These skills will also help run your life, too.

Tom wasn't born with these skills. He was fed the same negative B.S. that most of us are upon birth. "You can't be rich," "you can't do that," "success and power are for other people, not you," etc.... I have personally witnessed Tom overcoming his own personal head trash to become the leader he is today.

Once you implement the thought process and principles outlined in this book, your business and life will change forever. Mine has.

I am grateful that Tom introduced himself and opened my eyes to the 'real' business success formula: "Business is 10% math and 90% attitude." Most have this reversed.

Tom is the real deal. He is raw, authentic and uncomfortably 'in your face.' There is a lot of medicine that tastes like crap going down, but still works. This book is no different. If you drop your ego and put in the work, you will not only change everything in YOUR life; you will change the trajectory of your family tree forever!

Steve Shinholser

Foreword #2

I first met Tom Reber in 2002 when he jumped out of a beat-up Ford van, stuck out his hand while flashing me a killer smile, and said, "Hi. I'm Tom. I paint stuff." It was the first week of his new painting company *Reber Custom Finishes* and it was long before he thought about building a brand or knew how to grow a successful business. But I could tell right from that first meeting that Tom has "something special," drawing people in and making you root for him. Even still, I never would have guessed that this guy would go on to build a top-notch painting company and, more importantly, change tens of thousands of lives as the founder of *The Contractor Fight*. I never would have guessed that I'd be along for the ride.

Back in 2002, I owned a new residential remodeling company with my brother. Over the first few months after our initial meeting, just like he preaches, Tom was in full-on hustle-mode, relentlessly cold-calling me, "Do you need a painter yet?" "Hi. Me again. Do you need a painter yet?" Until one day I did.

Since then, Tom and I have gone on to work together, in one capacity or another through five or six separate businesses, almost non-stop for the last twenty years. I've been privileged to be there for many of the stories you'll read in this book. I've been witness to the highs and the lows of Tom's painting career, his business partnership, his first speaking gig after he sold his share of the painting business, the very first podcast episode, the first YouTube video, the birth of *The Contractor Fight*, and the thank you messages that roll in from the thousands of lives he's changed because of all his hard work.

I've also been witness to Tom's personal fight, the internal struggles and challenges he's overcome in the last twenty years to become the person who is qualified to write this book for you. Are Tom's struggles unique or extraordinary? Probably not. They're the same struggles we all share. The fight we're all fighting every day. The fight you may be fighting as you picked up this book.

In our social media world, as we watch our *friends'* highlight reels scroll by, we think our struggles are uniquely our own until you stumble on a Tom Reber video. Tom wears his heart on his sleeve and his passion for helping people comes shining through. He has a way of reaching through the screen, slapping you upside the head, and saying, "It's time to deal with your shit. It's holding you back. I want more for you...even if you don't."

I'm glad you've found Tom. I'm glad you've found your way to this book. After reading it, I'm sure you'll be inspired to build a better life for yourself and your family. I know I'm a better person for having him in my Life and I'm looking forward to our next adventure together. Whatever it is.

See you around *The Fight.*

~Neil Kristianson

Introduction

I did everything I could to not work in the trades.

My dad worked in paving, seal coating and then, finally, as a tile setter. He was always tired, dirty and never made much money. I grew up in Wheaton, IL and almost all of my friends had dads who were Doctors, Lawyers, Engineers…you know, important people who made a lot of money.

They went on frequent vacations and didn't work all the time, like it seemed my dad did.

Almost every contractor I saw growing up had a similar lifestyle defined by one word, "broke."

To be fair, we never really know someone's financial situation viewing it from the outside. A small house and older vehicle doesn't mean they don't have money. A huge house, new car and frequent vacations doesn't mean they're wealthy. You know this. I know this. But at the time, as a kid, I took all this as evidence that the trades were probably not the best option if you wanted to make money.

Not having a lot of money was tough enough. Another thing I saw was a lack of respect for those who worked in the trades. Again, my perception at the time.

My Uncle Roy got me into painting. He's like a big brother to me. We'd jam tunes, drink a few beers and have a lot of laughs. He was one of the very few contractors I saw that actually made money and had nice shit.

One day, a wealthy client of Uncle Roy's – a woman who had known him for almost 20 years - called him into the room where she was. Not a big deal, right?

"Painter. Can you come in here please?"

Instead of using his name. The name she had known for two decades, she called out, "Painter. Painter. Come here, please." What a slap in the face!

That experience, combined with the looks my dad would get showing up to my school functions filthy from busting his ass all day burned into me the story that those who work in the trades were not respected.

All these experiences - and my perception at the time -told me that it was the losers who went into the trades. If you wanted to crush it in Life, don't work in the trades. If anything, the trades are a good fallback option.

At the time of this writing, I am 51 years old. As I look back at my take on these experiences, I now see how insecure I was. My desire to avoid the trades (which I never did) was based on my own lack of being comfortable in my own skin. I didn't know who I was. I have since learned that success doesn't care what you do for a living. If you show up with your mind right, eyes bright, chin high and focused like a beast on taking daily action toward your goals… you will win.

My view of the trades, and my insecurity taught me a ton about the danger of defining success based on other people. Instead of identifying who I wanted to be and what success was to M.E., I fell victim to the comparison game. Every time we compare ourselves to someone else's success, we pound a nail in our own confidence coffin.

I've learned, and honestly am still learning to really be me. I am still a work in progress. I try to live unafraid and never hide who I really am and what makes me happy. I have learned to live a life that will lead to me respecting myself first. If I respect myself and show up in ways that make me proud, then I might earn the respect of other people. And, if they don't respect me, oh well!

That's one thing I hope for you as well. Can you look at yourself in the mirror each day and respect yourself?

"The Contractor Fight" is what I call the battle between your ears. We all have stories and experiences that have formed us into who we are. We are what we think, and the battleground is our mind.

The Fight is not with the people you think are 'cheap customers.' It's not with the unlicensed competitors or the "illegals," as many contractors think. The Fight is with yourself.

Sadly, most of the struggles contractors have are self-imposed. It's friendly fire. The negative ways we think about ourselves and our worth… friendly fire. The growing debt, working too much, small bank account… friendly fire.

Tom Reber

Winning the Fight is a choice.

You're noble and full of integrity. You bend over backward to serve your family and clients. You have taken it on the chin more times than you can count. Now, it's time to get yours. Earn what you're worth. Create a business that serves you and energizes you instead of one that beats you down.

Choose to own your crap and get better today.

This book was written to equip you to win the battle between your ears. There are stories, good and bad examples, and strategies to help you get a little better. One thing I tried to avoid was the typical 'this is how I made it' book. I wanted to avoid a book with a bunch of tactics and instead share some of my mindset and philosophies that have served me well and have guided thousands of contractors around the world to great success at home and in their businesses.

My intent is to teach you to think a little differently and trust that you'll apply whatever resonates with you to your Life and business.

Tom

Chapter 1: Own Your Crap

I Rode the Short Bus

The Twinkie Bus pulled up in front of my house and opened its door. I walked onto the bus, sat down, and noticed it was about half-full of the "special kids." There were kids in wheelchairs, kids with uncontrollable drooling who were making weird sounds, other kids making loud and intimidating outbursts and cries….and, me. This was quite the change for me as we rode to my elementary school.

I remember the bus pulling up to the school, getting out and wanting to run to the playground to hang with my friends, but I was redirected into the building with my new friends and into our classroom. I recall the looks I got from the "normal" kids on the playground as I got off that bus. It was clear that I wasn't normal anymore.

I don't know all the reasons why I was put into the Special Education Unit in my school, but I do believe it was out of

1

love. Word on the street is that I was an active child. We called it being "hyper."

I believe my parents did what they thought best and were advised to do at the time. It wasn't until I was thirty - and just becoming a father myself - that my Mom told me I wasn't put in there because I was "stupid" or "special," but that I learned things so quickly that I'd get bored and cause trouble in class. They didn't know how to handle me, so they decided to put me in the special education class.

Either way, I wound up on a bus and in a room for a couple years that told me I was stupid. That's how I took it. I wasn't smart enough to be in the normal classes with the normal kids; I needed to be with the kids who I believed - at that time - were mentally deficient.

This wired my brain in ways that would have me telling myself a story for the next few decades that I was dumb. It told me I didn't have what it took to compete intellectually in the world.

Why am I sharing this with you?

Simple. I chose to believe the bullshit for a few decades, and I still struggle with this bullshit from time to time.

"You can't learn this...you're slow."

"You'll never be able to communicate your true thoughts in real-time with someone, so just stuff it and move on."

"Don't set a goal too high because you probably won't be able to figure out how to get there."

*"You're too stupid to understand Money .... Business ....
People .... The World."*

These are some of the actual thoughts that run through my
mind.

I can choose to listen to this and believe it as true, or I can
take control of my thoughts and find a way to win.

I had to own the truth that I was hijacking my own success
for over thirty-five years because I chose to listen to the
bullshit voices.

Somewhere over the past few years I heard a phrase that has
resonated deeply with me.

"There is no progress without truth."

Loosely translated in Reber, that means, "Own Your Crap."

Does your marriage suck? Own your crap and chose to deal
with it.

Can't seem to keep an employee for longer than a month or
two? Own Your Crap. Be humble. Get coaching. Learn to be
a leader.

Maybe your business is barely scraping by again, the way it
has been for the past 13 years. Own Your Crap.

There is no progress in any area of your Life without first
telling yourself the truth. You are in control. Good. Bad. It's
you, and you alone.

Why Owning It Works

I naturally want to protect myself and make myself look good. Don't you? We will look for anything or anyone to keep us from being the reason we're not as successful as we'd like to be. As long as we don't have to claim responsibility for our results, we can play the victim card.

I have been blessed to see so many contractors change their lives in a short period of time by simply looking in the mirror and claiming responsibility for their situation.

True ownership is just that. You claim sovereignty over the garbage that is keeping you from winning. Anyone can acknowledge their crap, the true #fw (Fucking Winner) plants his flag there and kicks its ass. Owning Your Crap is about taking back the power you have given away for so long. The "I'm stupid," story that I believed about myself was the cowardly terrorist that was sabotaging my own freedom and success. For a few decades I tolerated it. I refused to put myself in situations that would challenge the little bastard.

Run Into the Punch

For about three years I was invited to be part of this non-profit event where there were some really powerful dudes. Guys who have accomplished some crazy stuff in their lives and businesses. The leadership event was also an event for a certain college fraternity. A.K.A.- "smart people." I was invited to be part of this thing for three years and for three years I didn't go.

I would tell myself, *"Tom, there's all these smart people there. You're starting this new career in your life as a coach and your resume isn't as impressive as these other guys going. You don't belong there."*

That was the general version of the story I told myself each year. And each year I avoided going with some lame excuse.

Until the year I went.

At some point I woke up. At some point I told myself to "run into the punch." I reasoned that I would never shake this "I'm stupid" thing unless I went toe to toe with it. As long as I chose to not fight, I would remain powerless.

So, I took action and booked my flight and a few weeks later I arrived at the event ready to rewrite my future.

About one minute into the first day of the week-long leadership event I was ready to bail. Somehow, I made the cut to be a breakout speaker and a panelist for this event and saw my bio was hanging on the wall as I walked in. It basically said, "Marine Corps Veteran and built a painting company." The other speakers had really long and impressive resumes. Things like "billionaire" and founder of "insert really well-known company here" as well as the fancy degrees after their names.

I couldn't have felt more unworthy of being on that wall listed as a speaker.

Immediately, the bullshit stories started rolling around in my head and I wanted to leave. But I chose to claim ownership over my fear. I chose to be the builder of the future I wanted to have. I went toe to toe.

I planted my fucking flag.

A couple hours later, I sat on the stage with a few impressive people as questions were asked of us. Before I ever offered any of my leadership or business knowledge, I simply said to the room of over a hundred young and bright men, *"Hi. I'm Tom. I didn't go to college. I have this fear that I'm stupid. I hope I can share something this week with you that helps you get a little better."*

We did our short Q & A session and afterward, the attendees were invited to go to a certain part of the resort and hang with the panelists. My mind was blown when I realized that about a third of the attendees showed up to talk to me. Apparently, they wanted to pick the brain of the stupid guy with the least amount of accomplishments hanging on the wall. Who knew?

There were many interactions that happened that week that were crucial to me fighting against my head trash. Many victories were had. Nobody else knew what I was fighting inside my mind that week. Nobody else knew that a few years earlier I filed a personal bankruptcy that also fed into the, "You're a dumbshit and a fraud" battle going on in my mind. Nobody else knew that almost everywhere I looked in my Life at that time I simply saw evidence of my lack of smarts and inadequacies.

But, I chose to plant my flag and Own My Crap.

I chose to face the thing that at the time scared me the most and I went to this event. I chose to get over myself and not look for my confidence through comparison to others, but instead embraced the reality that my path had formed me into a good man capable of succeeding in greater ways. I chose to tell myself that I was intelligent. I chose to look for evidence that I was on the right track.

Over the next several chapters you will be taught many strategies and tactics to help you reach the success you want. But, none of it will have the impact it is meant to have if you don't get your mind and heart right. I hope you'll take the time to look in the mirror and Own Your Crap. You may be broke and struggling to pay your bills. You may be kicking ass in your business. I don't know for sure where you are, but I promise you that if you don't seriously deal with your shit, you will never accomplish what you're meant to accomplish.

What do you need to own?

Tom Reber

Chapter 2: Get Oxygen

If you've ever been on an airplane, you've heard the flight attendant give the speech about the oxygen masks.

"In the event the cabin loses pressure, your mask will drop down...."

They also make sure to tell you, "If you're traveling with a small child or infant put your mask on first, then the kids."

Initially, if you're like most of us you think that's nuts.

Why would I not take care of my kid first? That's selfish of me to put my mask on first.

But the direction is solid.

You're no good to your kid if you don't have Oxygen getting to your brain.

The F.A.A. (Federal Aviation Administration) has a little chart that says if your plane is traveling at the average cruising altitude of about 33,000 feet, you have between 30-

60 seconds of what they call 'time of useful consciousness' if the cabin loses pressure.

Time of useful consciousness.

That's 30-60 seconds of you being any good to anyone. You better get that damn mask on.

Oxygen is Pretty Important

A little reading on SpinalCord.com will teach you quite a bit about the importance of Oxygen to the brain. Some of the long-term effects of oxygen deprivation can include:

- changes in mood/personality
- difficulty with memory
- struggling to walk, write, or talk
- chronic pain
- difficulties with impulse control, development of addictions, aggressive behavior
- depression, anxiety, confusion

The bottom line is that we are not at our best when Oxygen is deprived. We are not as healthy as we can be for ourselves and sadly, we make things harder on those we love.

Enough of the medical talk. I'm sure you can see where this is going in regard to your business.

Money = Oxygen

Oxygen = Life

Lack of money produces all kinds of issues in the health of your business. Think about it. When you're short on funds you may be moody, have a hard time focusing, struggle to do everyday things like paying your rent or afford a meal out. You may have chronic financial pain, a tendency to turn toward addictive behavior, and in many cases, struggle with anxiety or depression.

Lack of money sucks the Life out of you.

I remember coaching an HVAC guy several years ago. The very first question he asked me was, "What's one thing you'd do differently if you started in business all over again?"

"Simple," I replied. "Make sure I have enough air for the long haul."

In his first year of business, we built a plan to make sure he got Oxygen first. He ended that year having paid himself about $4500 per month and he banked close to $75,000 so he'd have Oxygen if the economy took a dump. For him, that was about 8 months of business overhead and the $4500 per month he needed at home in order to breathe.

I'm blown away by how easy it is for us to not make money. In the spirit of being a good boss we make sure everyone else has Oxygen first. This is honorable. And even though I've never in my Life missed a payroll for the people I have employed, I think it's stupid. I believe the worst thing I can do is deprive myself of Oxygen.

Remember all the side effects of not getting air to the brain? I know that I am a better salesperson when I have Oxygen. I make better leadership decisions when I have Oxygen. I am more creative about solving problems when I have Oxygen. It is not selfish to make sure you're breathing.

So, how do we make sure we can breathe and still care for the people we employ? How do I make sure that my brain gets fed first? How do I not come across as a total ass toward all the people I am obligated to support in my company? These are all fair and valid questions.

We will dig into the formal business stuff regarding this in the coming chapters, but first, we need to deal with your mind. Over the years I have found when someone is struggling to breathe it often comes down to one of a few different mindsets they have about money. Unless these are addressed, you will struggle.

Making Money Doesn't Mean You're an Asshole

Many of us have head trash around making money. I remember driving a piece of shit Chevy I bought for $400 down I-88 outside of Chicago many years ago. I worked for my uncle who was a painting contractor. I had just left the Marines and didn't really have a plan for myself, so I moved back to Illinois and made $14 an hour painting.

I sat in traffic waiting for my turn at the toll booth and there was this dude in a Mercedes next to me. He had a perfect car. He had nice clothes on that weren't dirty and he had perfect hair. He looked important.

He was a fucking asshole.

I never met him. He never looked my way. But I hated him. Somewhere in my Life I learned that having money meant you were a dick. So, I hated this guy.

I worked in homes for people who had money and I often found what I was looking for…assholes.

I brought my own mindset baggage to these people and thought that because they had money, they thought less of me. So, when I was around them, I saw nothing but arrogant assholes.

I've thought a lot about how I learned to despise people who made money and one memory keeps coming back.

I grew up in Wheaton, IL and lived with my dad throughout my high school years. He never made much money, even though we didn't lack for anything. Many of my friends had parents that were lawyers, doctors and people with other important titles and big paychecks. They lived on the other side of town in really big houses where everyone wanted to hang out.

We lived in a rented 1000 sqft ranch on the other side of town.

One of my friends from the football team was going through some family issues and needed a place to live and we offered to take him in. It looked like it was a 'go' until one of my rich friends made the same offer. Our friend went to live at the other place, and it hurt. I blamed it on the fact that we had a small house, not much money and it wouldn't have been as fun for him.

Looking back now, I believe the other house was the right place for him to be. But, at the time it hurt.

So, when I saw the rich guy in the Mercedes, I hated him.

Many of us make judgments about people who make money for whatever reasons we've given ourselves throughout the years. The point here is simple: Making money doesn't make you an asshole. Being an asshole makes you an asshole. Money is an amplifier of what you already are.

Don't deprive yourself and your family of the blessing that can come with money because you're afraid it will make you a dick. There are plenty of assholes in the world who are broke too. Money has nothing to do with your Asshole Factor.

Making Money is Possible

I didn't grow up ever thinking I could make money. And, even though my mom, dad, uncle and many people around me had started and run businesses, I never once thought I could start a business. I never thought I had what it took. And I certainly never believed I could make money. The personal development experts would tell you that I didn't believe I was worthy of it.

Getting the Oxygen you need and want starts with believing it's possible. So many people are telling themselves harmful stories that are sabotaging their financial future.

"Nobody in my family has ever made much money."
"I'm not good with money."
"I will never be rich."

On and on we bullshit ourselves. Guess what? You get what you look for. Whatever you tell yourself will eventually come to be. You're attracting that shit into your Life.

Instead, flip the story. When you feel yourself about to say or think something stupid, self-correct.

"I'm developing my money skills and getting better each day."

"I've made so many money mistakes, but I'm excited to be learning and growing so I can change my future."

"I'm putting in the work and implementing the actions needed because I'm on my way to being financially rich."

This isn't a "self-improvement, deal with your upbringing issues" book. I'm sure there are better ways to make this point. But, damnit…it is possible for you to make life-changing money.

Is it another $500 a month that would impact your Life? It's possible.

Maybe you want to break the six figures personal income level? It's possible.

Want to earn more in a month than anyone in your family ever earned in a year?

It is possible.

I've found that one of the biggest enemies of our success is the lack of mental discipline we have. Start feeding your mind healthy thoughts. Hang with mentally strong and positive people. When you see yourself going in the tank mentally, catch yourself and tell yourself you have what it takes.

Making Money Makes Everything Else Easier

Your personal life and your business will have many problems. That is a fact. Cars will break down, kids will break bones, your house will need fixing, your spouse will lose their job, employees will quit, clients will complain about quality on occasion, the taxman will come knocking, etc… All of these things, and more, are coming.

Dealing with them is easier when you have money. In fact, money will make several of these problems go away, or at the very least, make them appear smaller.

In fact, as I write this paragraph, I received a call from an attorney who says I owe $532.68 for an insurance policy for one of my old companies. It's a long story, but the bottom line is I didn't know I owed any money. We moved. I don't remember seeing a bill. My bad. The insurance company hires a debt collector, and the dude calls me to get me to pay up.

$532.68 is not a big problem because I'm focused on getting Oxygen. This is real Life.

Maybe you are having a hard time finding a #fw (fucking winner…aka A Player) to add to your team. Or maybe you need a right-hand person to help you manage jobs or run the office? It's easier to find that person when you have money. You can attract better talent and retain that talent when you have money.

Money does not equal happiness, but having it is certainly better than not having it. As a business owner, you are going to get jacked in the teeth many times throughout the life of your business. The good news is that you can pick the problems you have. You can choose to not have a money problem by implementing many of the mindsets and strategies I will lay out in this book.

One of my Battleground Programbusiness partners, Steve Shinholser, gives us a weekly reminder: "Don't mess with the money."

In other words, don't let anything in your business come before getting Oxygen. Oxygen is Life. The more Oxygen you have, the better you can care for your business, your people, and your clients.

Tom Reber

Chapter 3: Carry a Light Pack

I first hiked in Colorado in the summer of 2013. My friend Jeff and a couple of his buddies were going to hike a trail near Breckenridge and asked if I wanted to go. I jumped at the chance. The morning of the hike we were packing for the 13-mile journey that would reach an elevation of about 13,000 feet. I watched these experienced hikers carefully load their packs with items they needed. The thing that struck me was that they each loaded their pack to the 'ounce.' Not the 'pound,' but the 'ounce.' On the contrary, I literally packed about 5 gallons of water and food for 3 days in my pack. I had the heavy pack!

Being from the flatlands of Illinois, I had never heard anyone talk in terms of ounces, so this caught my attention.

What I didn't realize at the time was that these few moments of gear loading would serve as an example I would use for years to come about how to have a healthier business. These experienced hikers taught me that it's better to climb a mountain with 20 pounds on your back rather than 200 pounds. And that you should only bring things you will need for the trip.

This is the total opposite of what I see most contractors do when they are climbing the mountain of business success. They load themselves up with crap they don't need and opt themselves into carrying the 200-pound pack. What most don't realize is that every additional 'ounce' will require them to work harder to reach the top.

Overhead

My definition of overhead is:

"Whatever you need to write a check for in the business each month, even if you don't have any projects to do."

Need to pay the cell phone bill? Yep. You do even if you don't have a deck to build.
Your shop rent is due even if you don't have a ceiling fan to install.
The Oxygen you need to support your family (aka your salary)? You got it. That's overhead.

Overhead is not necessarily good or bad, it just is. One key to profitability is discerning what is really needed. One question to help determine whether or not an overhead expense should be allowed in the business is "How does this make me money?"

Marketing money is overhead. Does it make you money? You should know.

My bookkeeper is overhead. Does she make me money? Yes, she does if you have the right one on your team.

Sadly, most contractors don't know what makes them money and loses them money. This is why I focus so much on educating people on the numbers.

When we adopted my son Tiga from Haiti I saw a sign hanging in the orphanage that said, "To our guests: If there is anything at all you need while you're here, please let us know and we will show you how to live without it."

Struggling to make money? Start with emptying out your pack. You can live without more things than you think.

A Break-Even Crash Course

This part of the book can go one of two ways: I open your eyes and change your Life, or I confuse the shit out of you. The first time I was taught this stuff I was confused. But hang in there and keep learning. Just like anything else, if you put in the work, you will get it.

Let's start at the top of the business, where the money comes in:

You sell a job for $10,000. This money is called revenue-it's what you collect and deposit into your bank.

Next, what does it cost you to produce the work? That's the cost of your guys in the field, materials, permits, renting equipment, etc. These costs are called Costs of Goods Sold (COGS) or Direct Costs. This is money you would not spend unless you had a job to do.

Pretend your COGS on this $10k job are $6,000. That's 60% of the sale price.

The money left over is called your Gross Profit. $10,000-$6,000 = $4,000.

Your Gross Profit is $4,000 or 40% of the sale price. This percentage is important because it will determine whether or not you can pay your overhead (bills to keep the business open). In my world, Gross Profit is what you have left over to pay to keep the business open.

Let's also pretend that your monthly overhead is $10,000 per month. That includes your Oxygen, marketing, phones, insurances, etc...things that you need to pay no matter what.

Your Break-Even point is the amount of revenue you need to bring in and produce at your average Gross Profit percentage that will leave you enough money to pay the overhead and nothing more, thus 'breaking even' on your overhead.

Here's the break-even formula:

Overhead/Gross Profit Percentage $10,000/.40

In this case $10,000 divided by 40% is $25,000.

You'd need to sell and collect $25,000 and produce it at a 40% gross profit in order to have $10,000 left over to break even on your overhead.

Remember that in this example, this company is spending 60% of the sales money on producing the work.

60% of $25,000 is $15,000. That's what the company is paying to get the work done. The money left over is for overhead and anything above that, N.E.T. Profit.

If you've listened to The Contractor Fight Podcast, watched Contractor Fight T.V. or heard me speak, you have most likely heard me say, "Get at least 50% gross profit on your projects."

Here's why...as Gross Profit percentage goes UP, the amount you need to sell and collect to break even goes DOWN.

Back to our example.

$10,000 in Overhead/.50 (a 50% gross profit) = $20,000 needed to break-even.

Simply by raising your Gross Profit by ten points, you lower what you need to sell and produce by $5,000.

There are two numbers that will determine how hard it is to carry your pack. The first, is obviously your Overhead. The higher yours is, the harder the climb. The second number is your Gross Profit. We will dig into that in Chapter 4 when we talk about pricing and producing for a profit.

The Key to Winning the Overhead Game

Your budget.

The 'B' word. If you're anything like the thousands of contractors I've worked with and spoken to, the whole idea of a budget is intimidating. Maybe you sucked at Math in school. Maybe you come from a family that did a lousy job handling money. Maybe the idea of being disciplined screws with your ego because you want to be free to do what you want with your money.

Who knows?

But here's the deal. Those who run their business with a budget have Oxygen. Those who don't are usually suffocating.

If the word 'budget' is hard for you to grasp, then change it out with the word 'plan.'

We're contractors. We like plans.

Think of building a home. At some point, someone has a vision for what they want to build and puts it on paper. Then, someone does some figuring out of what is needed to pull it off. Finally, it gets built.

Your Money Plan (budget) is no different. You have a vision of what you want your business to look like. It's a dream that you map out on paper. Next, you figure out what you need to make it happen, and then you execute the plan with discipline.

For example, maybe you want to put $200k in your pocket each year. That's your personal Oxygen Number. It allows you to pay for your Life, bank some money so you can pay for your daughter's wedding and not go into debt when the dishwasher breaks, and so on.

Your Money Plan will literally tell you what needs to happen in order for you to get to the point that you can write that check to yourself each month. All you need to do is follow the plan.

The plan will guide you. It will tell you what you can afford when you can hire next, and what it will take to build your business the right way.

Another way I think of a budget is like a game plan. I coached High School Football for 17 years. Each week when we face an opponent we go into the game with a plan. We want to run certain plays in certain situations. We have a goal of getting so many yards rushing or a certain player the ball so many times.

The money plan is what you plan on spending that month on certain things to operate the business. Then, when your bookkeeper reconciles your accounts, pays the bills and gets everything current, you take the Profit & Loss Report for the month, and you compare it to what you planned to do. You actually look and see if you carried more weight than you planned on carrying.

This is where you realize that you had nothing planned for lunches, but you spent $400 that month on beer and wings!

This is where you notice that you planned to spend $3,500 on marketing and actually stroked a check for $4,200.

The number one priority of your business is to make money. It's not to do the trade you do. You can't consistently make money, nor can you reach your goals without a plan. Most contractors don't have a budget and the result is that they spend more than they should on stuff they really don't need. Making sure you don't load yourself up and burden your business starts with that plan.

Overhead expenses should really be viewed as investments. It should be items that are crucial for the journey. If what you're spending money on doesn't put revenue in at the top of the business or create more profit at the bottom of the business, it should be cut. Most companies have at least 3-5% of their overhead expenses being spent on stuff they don't use or need. Maybe you are paying for a software subscription that you bought at 2:30am last winter when you were broke and struggling? You thought this software would be the savior of your slow winter and now you're paying $97 per month, and you don't use it.

I once had a storage space for my business that was $200 each month. I literally forgot I had it. I hadn't been there in over a year!

Take some time to sit down with your bookkeeper and go through ever single item that you have been spending money on and be ruthless as you lighten your pack.

Oh, you don't have a bookkeeper? Get serious about this business thing and hire one.

Chapter 4: Price & Produce for Profit

Bill was an attorney who was acting as the General Contractor for his own house. I was out prospecting for work during the fall of my first year in business. I was hungry and spent hours every day handing out cards, knocking on doors and calling numbers on the sides of trucks.

I struck gold when I found out that Bill didn't have a painter for his 6,000 square foot brand new home. I thought I struck more gold when he agreed to hire me for $28,000 to paint it.

The best thing about selling a $28,000 job when you're in your first year of business is the excitement you feel! This was the largest contract I had signed, and I was certain this project would help move my business to the next level.

Fast forward a year later.

Bill was his own G.C. Bill didn't have a clue. There were delays, subs walked off the job and there were more delays.

The job that was supposed to take me a few weeks took over a year.

I didn't have a clue either. The job cost me $45,000 to produce. If you're remotely in touch with how math works you can see how selling a job at $28,000 that costs $45,000 to do is a problem. Forget the stress of dealing with this moron for over a year. Forget the fact that he called me on Christmas morning to bitch about his stain color. Forget that I couldn't get any of my painters to want to go back there and do the work.

Put all that aside and just look at the math.

$28,000-$45,000 = -$17,000

Basically, I paid $45,000 to paint Bill's beautiful new house and he only threw in $28,000.

Who's the moron?

I wish I could tell you this was a one-time thing, but I'd be lying. During the first few years of business, I made many estimating, pricing and production mistakes that cost me tens of thousands of dollars.

The Production

This chapter is titled "Price & Produce for Profit." Price is listed first. In fact, most of us start with our price, don't we? We look at a job and think, "Huh, the going rate for something like this is….," and we sell the job at a number that we think is right.

This is jacked up, which is why I will talk about what to charge later.

In order to make a profit you must know what it costs you to produce the work. This is your Costs of Goods Sold (or Direct Costs) to do the work. We need to start here or else everything else is a mess.

How much money do YOU get to pay to paint the house?
How much money do YOU get to pay to build the addition?
How much money do YOU get to pay to finish the floors?

The key words in those sentences are "YOU get to pay."

If you want to make a profit you must know what it takes to do the work. The labor, materials, permits and anything else it is going to cost you to get the job done.

Whatever that number is, is your reality. Don't get emotional about it. Don't try to lower it. It is what it is.

Show Your Work

If you struggle with knowing your numbers and true costs to do a project, I want to encourage you to use a super simple method to get it right. Break every job into 3 phases.

Phase 1: Pre-Job Preparations
Phase 2: The Build
Phase 3: The Finish

This system will help you to methodically think through each estimate you do and ensure you account for all of your costs.

Phase 1: Pre-Job Preparations is all about the time and money you will spend to get the job ready. This is running around picking stuff up, drive time, setting up the job site and 'prepping' the areas for the 'work.' It can mean whatever makes sense for you.

Phase 2: The Build is doing the actual work. You're painting the room or installing the doors.

Phase 3: The Finish is closing out the job. This is clean up, final detailing, client walk-throughs, etc.

When you add up the labor costs and material costs for each phase, you will have your estimated Job Costs for the project.

Let's break it down to install hardwood floors in an 1800 square foot home (PS-this is meant to be incredibly simple and I'm not a flooring guy).

Phase 1:

Man-hours to go meet with the client to make selections: 4
Man-hours to go get materials: 6
Cost of pre-finished hardwood: $12,500
Cost of your labor: 10 man-hours x $30 per hour = $300
Total Phase 1 Costs: $12,800

Phase 2:

Man-hours to remove/mark baseboards, tear out old floors, unload new floors: 24
Man-hours to prepare the sub-floors: 8
Man-hours to install new floors: 48
Cost of your labor: 80 man-hours x $30 = $2400
Cost for dumpster for old floors: $300
Total Phase 2 Costs: $2700

Phase 3:

Man-hours to re-install baseboards: 4
Man-hours to clean up, address any issues, load trucks and client walkthrough: 16
Cost of your labor: 20 man-hours x $30 = $600
Total Phase 3 Costs: $600

Total Cost to Me (the contractor): $16,100
This is what my company gets to pay to do the job. Regardless of what I charge, this is what I'm on the hook for.

This is what it is costing me to produce the work.

The Price

"What should I charge for this project?" This is easily the most common question asked in The Contractor Fight Facebook Group. Sadly, most of us put our ear to the ground to find out what the 'going rate' is and then price it similarly. Here's the issue with that: Most contractors have zero clue what they should be charging, so we're all basing our pricing off of someone else's wrong numbers. Giving a shit about the 'going rate' is financial suicide for you.

There's a lot to knowing your numbers, but we're going to keep it simple. This one thing is the fastest and easiest way for you to make more money immediately.

It will require two things:

1. You must know your costs to do the job.
2. You need to have guts and commit to this.

Tom Reber

Price your work to make a 50% Gross Profit. Remember, gross profit is the Sale Price - What it Cost You to Produce the Work in the Field (COGS). If you sell at $10,000 and it costs you $7,000 to produce the $3,000 left over is your gross profit.

Gross profit pays your overhead and final, or N.E.T. profit.

The higher your gross profit, the easier your financial life.

Let's use our hardwood floor estimate from above and price the job to make 50% gross profit.

The total cost to the contractor is $16,100. That is what we are estimating (guessing) it will take to do it right without any issues. Take our proposed job costs and multiply by 2. Then, sell it at that price or more.

$16,100 x 2 = $32,200

$32,200 is what the client gives you. That's the number you need to get to make a 50% gross profit.

"Tom, I'll never get that in my area….my trade." I can hear many of you now making excuses why it won't work for you because you're situation is 'special.'

You don't have to do this. You can continue to be one of the stressed and underpaid home improvement contractors who will never turn the corner in his business. It's your call. All I know is that I have hundreds of contractors in every trade selling and producing at 50% or better every day and in every part of the country.

I'm telling you that if you're delivering a great service and great experience for your clients that you deserve to make a respectable profit. Stop caring about what your competition is charging or about the clients that tell you that you're too expensive. Grow in your confidence that your number is right and fair for you and the client. Because you're charging more you can give more value to your client instead of trying to rush to the next job to make some money.

There's nothing worse than being busy and broke. Charge appropriately and be an uncommon contractor.

The Profit

The reason we need to price and produce properly is to have a solid gross profit. Without a high gross profit, it will be harder to pay for the overhead your company has. Your overhead eats three meals a day and snacks often! Meaning, money goes out of your business everyday just to stay alive. Your job is to sell and produce work at the highest gross profit possible in order to pay for your business to operate.

Gross profit is the difference between the sale price and the costs to produce the work. Having worked with hundreds of contractors I can say with confidence that most have a gross profit of somewhere between 20% and 35% until my team and I get our hands on them.

A 25% gross profit on that $10,000 job above means you have $2500 left to go toward the overhead. Running around for a 25%, 35% or some other low number is called the Hamster Wheel. Busy and not really getting anywhere financially. A low gross profit means you need to do more jobs in order to recover the overhead money. More jobs mean you need more leads coming into the business.

Check this out. Let's pretend you have an overhead of $18,000 per month and employ 3 guys in the field. You do all the selling and work very little in the field. Here's how gross profit impacts the business.

Sale Price	Gross Profit %	Gross Profit $	Jobs Needed to Pay for Overhead
$3500	34%	$1,190	15
$3500	43%	$1,505	12
$3500	50%	$1,750	10

I'll take the 50% gross profit option.

If you're like most people we show this to, you're sold on the importance of raising your gross profit. Once you're sold on the idea the natural question is "how do I raise it?"

You raise your gross profit one of two ways, or a combination of the two.

1. Raise your prices.
2. Lower your COGS (what it costs to produce the work in the field)

Let's look at how to do both.

Raising your prices is great in theory but we're often held back by a couple of things. First, our own belief that we can raise them. If you don't believe you can then you're right. That's why it's so important to develop your confidence about the numbers and the value you bring. That's why we spend so much time talking about your mindset and worth. Want to fast-track your mental adjustment? Job cost the last ten jobs you did. Most likely, you'll have a wake-up call.

You can raise your prices. You deserve to make money that is at least equal to the value you are delivering. Just because your competitors are cheap doesn't mean you need to play their game. Just because a client tells you that you're too expensive doesn't mean you are. Sure, maybe for them you are, but not to run your business right.

The second thing I see hold contractors back from raising their prices is that they suck at sales. They lack the skills. They think sales means you go out and 'wow' the client with all your knowledge and experience. Their presentation is a "brag fest" about how awesome they are. That is not sales.

One of the things we teach in our Battleground Program is that sales are connection. High-profit sales are the result of one human connecting with one or two others. Is your knowledge important? Of course, it is. Are your many years of experience important? Yes. But neither means jack if those things are not important to the client.

When you connect with the client and understand their reasons for buying you will immediately be selling at higher prices and raising your gross profit. We will dig into sales later in this book.

The second way to raise gross profit is by controlling your field costs. Labor is a huge profit leak if not controlled. I used to sell jobs at higher prices than my competition but did not make money because I didn't have a Job Plan. I didn't give scopes of work. I didn't put one guy in charge of running the job efficiently. I failed to communicate that the job was estimated for a certain amount of time. And the result was it took whatever they wanted it to take. Not because they're bad people, I was just a bad leader.

They also ran over the budget because of a thing called Parkinson's Law.

"Work expands so as to fill the time available for its completion"

If you don't give your crew a Work Order with clear expectations, they will almost always take longer than what you bid, cutting your gross profit. If you tell a guy, he has four hours to paint the room he will pretty much paint it in four hours. If you don't give him a time expectation, he will naturally fill the time available.

Give your team clear expectations.

You should also be having a weekly Operations Meeting where you pull the team together and debrief the jobs that were completed in the past week.

What was it bid at? How did we do? If we could do this job over again, how would we approach it?

This is called Job Costing. This will make sure your estimating side of the business is unified with the production side. I have a Job Costing sheet available for you at https://thecontractorfight.com/jobcosting if you want to grab it.

I cannot express the importance of a regular Operations Meeting. I've seen companies increase their gross profit by 10% in one month just by implementing this one thing.
Think of your price as one wing of an airplane and the production as the other. You need both to fly. Selling at the right price and then taking longer on the production means you'll crash. Producing the work efficiently with a sale price that is too low will mean that everyone but you, the owner,

will get paid. You want your wings to be in balance, with minor adjustments happening along the way.

Tom Reber

Chapter 5: Multiply Benjamins

I see a lot of articles, programs, and other content about 'doubling your business.' I get it. It's sexy to think about a business twice the size of what you have now. It's only natural for us to want to grow. In fact, if you're not growing you are dying. Unfortunately, when people talk about doubling their business, they almost always mean the top-line revenue or the number of people in the field producing work. Rarely do I hear them talk about how to double the things that really matter: Profit, time off, and contentment.

Do you want to double your overhead?

How about the number of average-performing employees working for you?

Do you really want double the sales?

What I have found is that when we find ourselves getting excited about 'doubling' the business it's usually our desire for something deeper that we really want. Think about it.

Why do you want to double your sales? Is it just to say you do x amount in sales or is there a deeper reason?

Hint: the deeper reason is that we think that by doubling our sales we will finally be able to pay ourselves the salary we want, or that we will have enough money to pay down the debt, or be able to take the time off we want.

You don't want the sales number.
You don't want more employees.

You want what you think those things will lead to: Freedom.

Freedom to spend your time how you want to. Freedom to be content with your Life and situation. Freedom to drop $250 on dinner for you and your wife and not give a shit.

Don't think I'm "poo-pooing" growing top-line revenues. It does make sense at times to put our sights on increasing sales or some other metric, but in my experience, we are better off putting the crosshairs on the actual true outcome we want first.

I want to multiply profit. I want to multiply freedom. When I work with contractors one on one, we spend a lot of time making sure we are outcome focused. How much of your time can we get back for you? Are we as profitable on each job as we can be? Are you enjoying your role in the business?

Let's iron those things out before we try and 'scale' the business. Let's make sure we are scaling the right stuff.

A guy called me recently to ask about our coaching programs. I asked him, "Why do you want help? What's going on in the business that made you reach out now?"

"I need to get to five million in sales!" he replied enthusiastically.

I listened to him go on about how important it was to reach that goal and then I asked what was so special about five million in annual sales.

"I want to pay myself $250k." answered my new friend.

"You can't pay yourself $250k unless you do five million?"

The 8 seconds of silence seemed like 8 minutes until he said, "I'm not really sure. That's a great question."

More of the sexy things doesn't always produce more of the things you really want. I have contractors that do 1.5 million and pay themselves $400k. I know guys who have 2 employees, pay themselves $175k and take every Friday off to hang on their boat...oh, and they only really work about nine months a year.

They are clear on multiplying the outcomes they most want.

Growing a big business that does 5, 10, 20 or 50 million is not wrong. I've worked with those who've done it and many of them have a good life and solid companies. But, for most of you reading this book, you're out there grinding away and working hard to provide for your family. You're not going to build a million-dollar business because only about 4% of small businesses actually ever hit that revenue mark.

Most of you want a future that includes making great money, being respected, having a life that you enjoy and not drowning in debt. That's what multiplying Benjamins is all about. How can we put more $100 bills in your pocket each week? How can we ensure you are multiplying the things that you really want instead of the headaches, stress, debt and frustrations that the average contractor experiences? Once your "Benjamins" are multiplying, let's turn those into "Clevelands!"

Set a Profit Goal

We already talked about getting Oxygen. That's paying you for the work you do in the company. Profit is different. To be clear, N.E.T. Profit is what is left after all other business expenses are paid.

The guys are paid. The materials are paid for. The overhead is paid…the shop rent, cell phone, marketing, your salary, etc. Everything that needs to be paid is paid. The amount left over is your N.E.T. Profit.

This is your financial reward for taking the risk of running a business. This is your 'Atta Boy' and pat on the back. This money can be used to reinvest into the business, hook up your team with bonuses, a nice bonus check for you, pay down your line of credit or whatever else you and your accountant decide.

What's left over is what matters.

Having a clear profit goal matters more than a revenue goal for most small businesses. For example, if your company does $50k per month in sales and we find a way to be 5% more efficient in the field, you will make more money than if you increased sales by 10%. I won't bore you with the math here.

A profit goal will ensure you are focused only on the most important outcomes instead of chasing the 'vanity' numbers.

It's been said "Revenue is vanity, Profit is Sanity & Cash is King."

You can't get to cash without first getting to profit.

Set a Lifestyle Goal

Eric is a painter I've known for years. I see him at industry events each year and the first thing I ask him is, "How many days?"

He usually replies with, "121," or some other figure in that range.

That's how many days a year he schedules to take off from his business. He likes to hike, run and travel. He doesn't let his business get in the way.

Many people think that you have to choose between the ideal lifestyle you want and making money. That you have to choose between working all the time and having money or working less but being available for the family.

That's bullshit. You can have both.

You can have time and money. You are in control of who you work for, when you work, what you charge, when you take days off and everything else in your business. I made a decision over 17 years ago that I wanted to coach high school football and I was blessed to do that for almost two decades. With the support of my family and business partners I have lived the life I wanted to live.

What lifestyle are you missing out on? How long has it been since you took a real vacation? Are you free to pursue passions that you have or are you a slave to the business?

You really don't have many choices to make. I know it may feel like you do, but you don't.

There are money choices and there are time choices and there are happiness choices. Don't overcomplicate things.

If the money is not where you want it, you make adjustments not excuses. Cut some fat from the budget and be disciplined in your spending. Set weekly sales goals and attack them. Set a profit goal on each job and hit it.

If your time isn't being spent where you want it spent, make adjustments. Talk to your spouse, partners, friends and anyone else who knows you well and figure it out. Put the things on your calendar that are important to you. Do that first. Need time with your daughter…put it on the calendar and honor it. So what if you need to get some work done. Figure out how to do the work without blowing off your kid. We find time for the things that are most important to us.

Are you unhappy? Then, make a choice to look inside of yourself and make the needed adjustments. What makes you happy? You honestly have control over your own happiness. It's not the external shit you think it is. For example, many think making more money will make them happy, when the truth is that what they really want is freedom. Pursue freedom. Make choices that are in alignment with who you want to be as a person.

Multiply what you want more of in your life and business.

Chapter 6: Show Me Your Friends

Many years ago, I was casually introduced to the idea that you become the average of the five people you hang out with the most.

Jim Rohn, entrepreneur, author, and motivational speaker, made that idea famous, and many have quoted him since. "You're the average of the five people spend the most time with."

Take a look around you. Do you see someone overweight? Chances are, their closest friends are too. See that girl with a cigarette in her mouth? I bet some of her best friends have one too. How about that one dude who makes $40-50k per month? He probably surrounds himself with people who make about the same.

Our mothers were right when they told us to choose our friends carefully. I have seen it so many times in my own life... I start to take on some of the habits, characteristics, and results of those I spend the most time with.

Many years ago, I started hanging around with Steve Shinholser. Steve spoke at an event about how to make more money as a Pond Contractor. He lit up the room with example after example of how he made millions. The attendees laughed at his jokes and were inspired by his "kick-you-in-the-ass" approach.

Immediately after the event, I made my way to Steve to introduce myself. Once I had him cornered, I said something to the effect of "Everything you said was spot on and great, but there's one problem." He looked at his new friend and business partner (neither of us knew that at the time. It took two more years before that happened) and said, "What's that?" "Their thinking." I said, "Very few of the people here will change a damn thing because their thinking is jacked up."

I was partially correct.

Yes. I believe the biggest thing that holds us back from the success we want is what happens between our ears. The stories we tell ourselves.

"I'm stupid."
"I'll never make that kind of money."
"That's not possible in my area...my industry."

What we think guides what we believe. What we believe drives our actions. Our actions produce our results. Good or bad.

Example: I tell myself that there's no way I can raise my prices. Not in my town! (thought). This becomes the story that I carry with me and repeat on autopilot (belief). This story keeps me from taking the one action of increasing my prices...(action) and, in turn, keeps me in the same financial situation I've been in with no hope of improvement (result).

Everything starts with our thoughts.

So then, why was I only partially correct? Simple. I was missing a crucial piece of the puzzle of success: Your Friends.

The reason so many of us struggle to make lasting positive change is that we lack the influence of people who live out positive success habits.

A few things happened after my introduction to Steve. First, he hired me to coach his new marketing guy Logan. Over that year and a half, Steve began to rub off on me...and me on him. This happened because we had a couple phone conversations each week about business stuff.

I started making more money. Steve started having a bigger impact on people.

We were influencing each other, and we weren't aware of it. At least I wasn't at the time.

Second, a couple of years later, we started this thing called the Contractor Sales Academy (CSA) because we wanted to help contractors get back their time and make the money they deserved. We wanted them to stop short-changing themselves.

There were many people who jumped into our new little company and made a choice to hang around guys like Steve and me. Those who made it a point to show up consistently improved pretty much every area of their lives. Those who didn't...haven't.

This is not a plug for our programs, although I believe every home improvement contractor should learn what we teach.

This is a real example that has played out in front of me over the past several years. I have witnessed hundreds of people reach greater success because of the relationships they have formed in our groups.

Who you hang out with matters to your health, marriage, business, and your bank account. Who you hang out with influences every area of your life, so be intentional.

Hard Choices

As we go through life, we will encounter many different people and build a bunch of relationships. What determines whether or not someone gets to be in your tight circle of influence? Remember, you're influencing someone else with your characteristics and habits, too!

Below are a few criteria I use to determine who I will spend time with. Special note: there are people in our lives who don't make the cut...an old friend, your cousin, existing friends, etc... Love them. Respect them. Just limit the amount of time you spend with them.

They Are Generally a Positive Human Being

Negativity is an anchor. It's like a bag of potato chips... you have one and then another until the bag is gone. That's how negativity works for me. If I'm not careful, I easily jump in and take part in the language of negativity. Remember the whole thoughts...beliefs...actions...results thing?

Life and business are hard enough. I'm looking for "the cup is half-full" people.

They Work on Themselves

All of us are fucked up to some degree. We have some habits we wish we didn't have. We know we can be better in certain areas of our lives. I get it. We are imperfect. If someone has some self-awareness about who they are and how they got where they are, and they make a decision to better themselves...that works for me.

I want to hang with people who are developing the habit of working to better themselves. Why? Because they know that they are not perfect the way they are like the world will tell them. They tell themselves the truth and they take steps to improve their situation. This is a habit that I want to be around.

They Call Me Higher

There are many reasons I am with my Queen. One huge reason is that she tells me the truth, no matter how uncomfortable it is for either of us.

"You need to stop being the weak link in this relationship." That's what she said to me after an incident where I was being a total douche.

That one hurt, but she was right. I am blessed to not only have her, but so many other people in my life who call me on my BS.

Hanging around a bunch of people who just let you do you, even when it's getting in the way of you being a better person and reaching the goals you have, makes no sense.

Sure. Be you. Just be better.

I value the people in my life who are in my corner and want me to grow. I value the conversations when I'm told the truth.

Who are you hanging out with? Who needs to be fired? Who needs to audition for your "five?"

How about the other way around? What value are you bringing to others? Are you the weak link? The one bringing negative influence to others?

Who we surround ourselves with is a choice. Choose wisely, and you will see huge improvements in every area of your life.

Chapter 7: The 'F' Word

I've been known to drop a few "F" Bombs in my time.

There's nothing like a well-timed "Fuck" with just the right tone behind it.

But, that's not the "F" word I'm talking about in this chapter.

Any guesses what it could be?

Fart?
Feelings?
Funny?
Fairies?
Frank?

You're not even close!

fa·nat·i·cal

/fəˈnadək(ə)l/

adjective

*filled with excessive and single-minded zeal.
"fanatical revolutionaries"

*obsessively concerned with something.
"he was **fanatical about** security at night."

This dictionary definition is pretty spot on if you ask me. Single-minded & obsessed totally make a case for me personally.

Obsession is a good thing when it comes to your success. Being excessive & single-minded in your commitment to something is not a bad thing.

Note: being obsessed & excessive can certainly be harmful in several ways that I hope I don't have to spell out here.

How much do you want to win? Sadly, many in our society 'talk' more than they 'do,' and the result is they underachieve and whine about how they're a victim.

For our purposes in this book, I want to spend some time on two main areas where being fanatical will help you reach your goals faster.

Clarity

Most of us set goals and have no idea why we picked that goal. For example, remember the guy I briefly mentioned a couple chapters ago who wanted to build his company to five million in revenue?

Me: Why five million?
Him: So I can pay myself $250k per year.
Me: The only way you can pay yourself $250k a year is to build a five-million-dollar company?

Him: I think so.

Me: What's so special about paying yourself $250k?

Him: It will allow me to get out of debt, take some trips, save for retirement and still pay all my bills. I'll be able to breathe.

Me: It sounds like you want freedom?

Him: Huh, yea.

Me: What if we could get you that freedom and bypass the whole building a five-million-dollar company and the mess that comes with that?

The five million and the two-fiddy were just a couple of vehicles to get him the freedom he wanted.

I said earlier most people set a goal without really knowing why. Too often, we set goals based on other people's opinions or their definition of success.

Clarity is king because when you have it, all the unnecessary shit falls to the side and allows you to give your time and energy to what you really want. Your own personal definition of success.

What do you want?

What do *you* want?

When you take the time to really dig and answer that question, you will then be able to avoid the BS that distracts and pulls you off course. You will be more efficient with your time. You will make each day count instead of spending it pursuing a ghost.

A great place to start getting clarity is to understand your non-negotiable values. Here's a possible list to get started.

Tom Reber

Non-Negotiable Values List

- Authenticity
- Achievement
- Adventure
- Authority
- Autonomy
- Balance
- Beauty
- Boldness
- Compassion
- Challenge
- Citizenship
- Community
- Competency
- Contribution
- Creativity
- Curiosity
- Determination
- Efficiency
- Fairness
- Faith
- Fame
- Family
- Friendships
- Freedom
- Fun
- Growth
- Happiness
- Home
- Honesty
- Humor
- Impact
- Influence
- Justice
- Kindness

- Knowledge
- Leadership
- Learning
- Love
- Loyalty
- Meaningful Work
- Openness
- Optimism
- Peace
- Pleasure
- Poise
- Popularity
- Recognition
- Religion
- Reputation
- Respect
- Responsibility
- Security
- Self-Respect
- Service
- Spirituality
- Stability
- Success
- Status
- Time
- Trustworthiness
- Wealth
- Wisdom

Read these words. Add your own. Read the words again and notice which ones wake you up a bit. Which words poke at your heart? Which resonates with you the most? Which ones make you come alive?

Make a list of the top ten. Then narrow it down to the top three. Set goals that are rooted in these three words, and you won't go wrong. This is your success.

You're now on your way to having clarity about what is most important to you...what you really want.

Your goals and actions should support these three words. For example, my mission and number one goal in The Contractor Fight is to bring respect and dignity back to the trades. That's what drives me. This was created from one of my non-negotiable values, impact. I value having a positive impact on those around me and in the world. This goal, bringing respect and dignity back to the trades, is at the center of all of our decisions in The Fight. It guides us. It's deeply rooted and unmovable because it is one of my top three. The goals that I set around this value are true and right.

Get clear on what you really want, and everything changes.

Consistency

You're clear on what you want. Your target is identified. But we all know that just because you say you want something doesn't mean it will happen. You've got to do some heavy lifting. You need to take some action.

Once these actions are determined, it will require consistency to move closer to your goals.

Be like water. Water cuts through the rock because it keeps showing up day after day.

Far too many people sabotage themselves because they lack consistency of action. They expect quick results.

"Hey, I've made 50 cold calls to prospects, and nobody has bought anything."

"I did company meetings with my guys for a couple months, and nothing changed."

Here are two foundational truths about winning the consistency battle:

1. You will not always feel like doing what you need to do.
2. You will not often see quick results.

I have so much respect for those who are consistent. It's not sexy. It's usually the mundane and boring things that move you closer to the wins you want.

Starting something new is fresh and exciting, and fun! Doing the same shit day in and day out over time is the challenge for most...and the most rewarding.

Let me give an example that is probably close to your heart as a contractor.

Finding kick-ass employees is a huge challenge for the trades right now. Most companies are selling a ton of work and are struggling to build teams to produce it.

"I need people!"
"I can't find any people!"
"Nobody wants to work!"

I can keep going with the complaints, but I won't.

Building your team is the same as building your brand and marketing your business. It requires consistent action. Here are a few things that it will require...these things done consistently over time will move the needle for you.

- Train your current employees and build a culture they want to be a part of, and invite their friends.
- Have regular team meetings recognize them, hold them accountable and have fun.
- Train current employees on how to spot potential hires.
- Run ads all the time.
- Hold your own Job Fair.
- Recruit 365 days a year...not just when you need people.
- Build your brand and continue to market...the more eyeballs on you, the better.

These are a few examples of how you need to show up consistently to get the result you want.

Newsflash: the people you want to work for you are already working for someone else. Be like water and they will eventually give you a little attention, and then you'll have a shot at stealing them from their current employer, who is probably not providing growth opportunities.

Clarity and consistency are the two most important words for success. Figure out what you want. Do the shit every day needed to move you closer to what you want.

Don't overcomplicate it.

What are your alternatives?

You can ignore the need for clarity and just try to succeed by working more and harder, hoping you land where you want.

You can refuse to be consistent in the high-impact activities and continue to underachieve and let yourself and those around you down.

I say you put your crosshairs on the right targets and do the damn work.

Many years ago, I started a podcast. Then, a YouTube channel. I had no clue what I was doing, but I knew my mission. I was clear. So, I showed up several hundred times and educated and shared my knowledge. This clarity and consistency have built the world's most impactful community of home improvement contractors. Getting clear and being consistent has helped tens of thousands improve their lives, grown my business, and led to a TV show on HGTV. There were and are days and weeks and even months when I don't feel like doing the work.

But success doesn't give a shit how we feel. It takes what it takes.

Tom Reber

Chapter 8: Tick Tock Goes the Clock

Cattle Call

It was a Saturday morning, and I was excited to go do the bid that had been scheduled by my office. The only time the prospects could meet was on Saturday at 9am. It wasn't ideal. In fact, it would require me to miss my son's basketball game. But I needed a sale and had a family to feed...so, I went.

On the way, I was pretty fired up. It was a whole house paint job that would end up somewhere around $35k. It was also a beautiful morning. The sun was out. My windows were down, and the music was jammin'!

You know those days, right? All seems bright and you're optimistic. There's nothing like having an opportunity to go bid on a nice-sized job. I felt like this project was a slam dunk since it came as a referral.

As I rounded the corner on their street, something didn't seem right. As I drove closer, I recognized a few of the other vehicles parked out front of the home. Three of my competitors just happened to be hanging out in front of the home, finishing their coffee and shooting the breeze. I parked and got out to say "hi" to my industry buddies. Over the next few minutes, as I talked with my painter friends, another four vehicles pulled up and parked. One van was lettered, and the three other vehicles were not.

Let's fast forward a bit. At exactly 9am, the homeowner opened the door and invited the eight of us in to talk about the paint job.

"Thanks for coming today. This was the most convenient time for us. We just closed on the house yesterday and need to move in by the end of the month. The first thing we need to do is paint the house."

She then handed out spec sheets of what needed to be done and even listed the materials and colors she wanted in each area.

"Go ahead and walk the house and figure up your price for the job. I figured this was the best way to keep everyone honest and get the best pricing for the job. Also, when you send the bid over later today, please explain why we should hire your company. We will then review all of the quotes and then make our decision by Wednesday night."

It was at this moment I realized that this was BS and I looked at her and said, "Lady, go pound sand! This is ridiculous," and I walked out, tossing her little job packet on the table.

Ok. That's what I wish I did. As I write this, I'm hoping there's a different outcome than the one that actually played out, but if there was, we wouldn't have this book!

It was a big job, and we were way better than our competitors. I was going to win this job. I diligently walked the home and figured every aspect of this job to the penny. I could tell she was an organized person, and I was going to wow her with my attention to detail in my quote. Two hours later, I left her home with several pages of notes that I was going to turn into the most professional and detailed estimate the world had ever seen. I was going to blow her mind!

I said goodbye with a little swagger because this job was mine and left.

I spent the next few hours at a local coffee shop putting together the world's most professional bid. I explained everything we would do, how we would do it, and why we would do it in the order we were going to do it. I even inserted pictures of her rooms and products we would use to do the job "right."

I shared about how we employed the best people...not a bunch of subcontractors like I knew most of my competitors did.

I shared how we were a better bet than the two General Contractors she had there that day to bid the job. I told her we were 'specialists' unlike those 'generalist' GC's who were probably going to sub it out to people they barely knew.

I shared about how we did background checks, trained our employees, and had won Small Business of the Year a year earlier.

After I put in about 6 hours of my life into this bid, not to mention a ton of soul, I hit send on my laptop.

Sunday Bloody Sunday

The next day, Sunday that is, I received a reply from my soon-to-be client. They had narrowed it down to four of us but needed some more information.

"Please break your bid down and itemize it by room and surface to be painted."

You heard that right. Every room. Every surface. Broken down by labor and material costs.

After another four hours that Sunday night, I hit send again.

At this point, I had spent about ten hours of my life tap dancing for this future client. I actually still felt optimistic about my chances.

I mean, come on... this is business. It's a competitive world out there and we need to make the case for why we're the ones to hire. We have to fight for these jobs and earn the work. This is just how it is in the trades.

Wednesday

They finally made their decision on Wednesday afternoon. I saw the new email sitting in my inbox and knew I won the job. I had the most professional and detailed bid, shared at least fifteen reasons why we were a good choice for the job, itemized everything the way they wanted, and I even made follow up calls on Monday, Tuesday and Wednesday to make sure they knew I was serious about winning their business.

"Thanks for the bid. We have decided to go with one of the other companies."

That was it. I lost. All that effort and nothing to show for it. Oh, well. This is the game. Next.

That story was one example of far too many bad experiences I had through the years. That scenario played out at least a thousand times in my life.

"Just leave the bid in the mailbox."
"Break it down, labor and material."
"You're twice as expensive as all the other bids we got."
"We can only meet on a weeknight after dinner."
"We need to think about it and get some more bids."
"I need to check with my financial planner first."

I'm sure you have your stories too. I'm sure you can add to the list of stupid things we hear in the sales process.

Stop Stealing from Your Family

This is a book about Winning the Contractor Fight, so I had to talk about the sales process. I have so much to say on this that I will probably write another book that is only about selling, but I'm going to share some foundational things here for you that if you let it sink in, and you implement, it will change your life.

The problem with most contractor sales processes is that they are not their processes. They are the prospect's process. We have been programmed to play by everyone else's rules all in the name of accommodating the prospect and working hard to earn their business. Their process involves running around town, meeting at times that are not the most convenient, typing bids up, itemizing those bids, and then hunting them down and hoping we can get a 'yes.'

The prospect's "process" requires crazy amounts of time, and often the result is that we steal from our families. We steal time and memories. We piss off our spouses because we miss dinner or need to go do a bid on a Saturday or Sunday or during dinner on a Thursday night. We also steal from ourselves. We don't work out as much and get fat...stealing years off of our lives. We give up our hobbies... stealing our joy.

We steal from our businesses too. Instead of investing our time on things that will move the business forward, we are stuck in the time-suck sales process. This steals money from the company.

I don't fault anyone for this. We do it because we want to provide for the people we love. We do it because this is how the game is played in the trades. You win some. You lose some.

Sadly, this process, the prospect's process, leaves most contractors too busy, unhappy and struggling financially.

But there is a different way. A way that will give you your time back. A way that will stop disappointing your spouse. A way that will grow your bank account. A way that will ensure that you never spend time in front of someone that will never be your ideal client.

Shin-Fu

Remember Steve Shinholser from the chapter called "Show Me Your Friends?" We started this little business in 2015 called the Battleground Program. It was born out of Steve's pathetic closing rate. Simply, put, he was tired of getting the runaround. He was tired of hearing your prices are too high after he spent hours in the sales process. He was sick of wasting time on the wrong people.

Keep in mind, Steve was already extremely successful. He built and sold a multi-million-dollar pool maintenance company, and his pond business was doing great. He was crushing it when it came to profit. He was just tired of playing the time-wasting sales game.

Steve and I took some things we learned about sales over the years and created a place where contractors could learn a different way. I'm not going into much detail about the CSA and its history here because we've since brought everything under the umbrella of The Contractor Fight. If you want to learn more about how to sell in ways that your competitors never will, head to thecontractorfight.com/battleground and check it out.

I only share this for you because most of you reading this need a different way to sell. Of course, I am my own biggest fan and believe that our Shin-Fu sales training is a no-brainer, but no matter what you do... create a process that serves you and doesn't steal from you.

Our time is the most valuable thing we have, and yet we willingly give it away to people who don't respect ours. We bend over backward for prospects just to be left holding nothing in the end.

If you're going to truly win the contractor fight, you need to take control of your sales process.

Here's the typical contractor sales process:

Get a Lead-->Schedule & Do an Estimate--> Tell Them How Great You Are as a Company-->Send a Bid-->Follow Up-->Get a Yes or No

We've done research and surveys over the past six years, and the average amount of time that this process (the prospect's process) takes is about four hours. Drive time, in-person meeting, writing the bid, follow up, et...

Our process looks like this:

Get a Lead-->Send us Pictures-->15-minute phone call to learn five critical pieces of information that will determine if we are a good fit and that we are on the same page with the money-->Deposit Check, Consultation Fee for a site visit, or we part ways and don't waste each other's time.

Marino paints cabinets. He shared with me that in 2020 he received 712 leads. He sold 110 of them for HIS PRICE. He did ZERO on-site consultations to sell those projects. He didn't spend any time playing the revision game. He didn't spend countless hours chasing people who went into the Witness Protection Program after they talked money. Total hours saved (he tracks this religiously) was 1400. That's 175 eight-hour days he saved by not playing the typical sales game. He invested the saved time taking better care of his clients, training his team, and enjoying his family and his life.

Let me also say that some of you are asking, "Wouldn't he have sold more jobs if he went out there in person?" Fair question. The short answer is "no." Stop playing the show up and pray game. The goal is not a high closing rate. The goal is to sell at 50% gross profit or better and to make sure you protect your time. Only those who qualify to be your client get an in-person visit.

This is one of hundreds of examples I can share with you about people who chose to sell a different way...Home Builders, Plumbers, Flooring Contractors, Electricians, Roofers, Remodelers, General Contractors, Window Dudes, Painters, Landscapers... it doesn't matter what you do, where you live or how your competitors do it. When you make a decision to no longer be everyone's little bitch, the game changes.

Here are a few thoughts and some advice I have as you decide to take control of your sales process. I promise you that this is one of the most important things you can do as a business owner.

1. People buy for their reasons, not yours. Find out theirs.
2. Not everyone is your customer. The faster you determine that, the more time you will save.
3. It's not your job to find their money. Stop revising your bids to fit what you think their budget is.
4. Stop going to meet people in person that don't already know what it's going to cost.
5. You are a human being who deserves to be respected. Don't allow anyone to steal your time.
6. The sale happens on the phone before you ever go meet them in person.
7. Sales is a skill that can be learned and developed. Nobody is a born salesperson.
8. There are five things your process should include: The Motive, The Money, The Truth, The Influencers, and The BS Meter. These are the five steps of the Shin-Fu. These are the things we want to know BEFORE we meet in person... what's important to them, what they are willing to spend, what will happen if I go meet you in person, who else needs to be on board with this job and how much it costs if I

come out and you don't sign a contract and give me a deposit.

9. Stop being a know-it-all and ask better questions. Your time will be saved, and your bank account will grow.

10. Roleplay. The more you practice, the better you will be when it matters most.

Most sales training programs talk about how to handle objections and raising your closing rate. That's nice. I get it. In fact, in the past, I was a student of many of those methodologies. When you learn to have the right conversation upfront on the phone with someone, you will connect with them in ways your competitors never will. Trust will increase. They will open up, and all those typical objections will become non-issues. Through the spirit of the conversation and learning a few cool ways to communicate with people, the objections you normally get will be addressed in the flow of the initial conversation.

As far as your closing rate goes... instead of tracking that, track your Effective Sales Rate (ESR). This is found by taking the dollars you sell in a period of time and divide it by the number of hours you spend in the process.

Example: You sold $75k this week. You went on 9 appointments, typed shit up, followed up, etc and spent about 36 hours this week selling the three jobs for a total of $75k. Your ESR is $2083.

The higher your ESR, the more efficient you are as a salesperson.

(Note-if you have a sales team and pay them any kind of salary you will want this number to be as high as possible).

I'd rather spend 15-20 minutes on the phone to find out everything I would find out in person. That's just me, though. I'm pretty protective of my time.

You're reading this book because you want to win more. I'm telling you now that the sooner you unfuck your mindset about how the sales game is played and won, the sooner you will drastically change your life.

You are one decision away from the freedom you want.

Tom Reber

Chapter 9: Marketing

Each year, sometime around the fall, I do a rant video and yell at contractors. I don't plan this rant; it just happens. I get bent out of shape because I start to get messages on social or through email that say things like:

"The year was going great, and then the work just stopped. Now, I don't know how I'm going to pay my bills."

"How can I get some work?"

"I need some quick ideas to get some leads."

Every year it's the same story, and it pisses me off. I'm pissed because this is preventable. This is friendly fire on your business.

The biggest mistake I see is that contractors stop marketing their businesses when they get busy. Spring hits, and the phone explodes. You can't keep up. Work is rolling in. Money is flowing. Life is good. So, your attention is no longer given to hunting and farming to generate leads and the result of this hits your business a few months later.

This is one of the reasons why your business doesn't grow. You don't make marketing a way of life. The reality is when you start a business your number one job is to get work. Not wearing your bags. Not designing the cool water feature.

Getting work.

You don't have a business if you don't generate quality leads that turn into sales.

The Champion of Marketing

Whether you do the marketing yourself or hire someone to do it, you must be the spearhead leading the way and ensuring your company doesn't slack off. Many of you will tell me that your work speaks for itself, and you've never had to advertise.

Good for you if you want to stay where you're at. If you want to grow your business and own more than a job, you will need to excel at creating and executing a kick-ass marketing plan.

There's no such thing as too many leads. When you have more than enough leads coming in, you have options. You can be picky. You can raise prices (as most of you should). You can sell with courage.

Market your company as though your life depends on it.

Strategy vs. Tactics

Most market their business by throwing things against the wall and hoping they work out. You try Facebook ads because someone said it worked for them. You sign up for things like Home Advisor or Thumbtack. You run an ad in some high-end magazine. You knock on some doors. You hire someone to post shit on your social media pages. Maybe some direct mail. Maybe some Google ads. You take the bait and hire that company that says they'll build you a website, manage it and also do your social media for $300/month. They promise you the moon and the stars, but a year later, you still don't have any leads, and you're stuck in a contract. Oh, and if you cancel, you lose the website because they own it.

Before you start trying things, take some time to create a real marketing plan that is rooted in strategy.

Build your marketing plan like this:

Goal-what you want to accomplish
Strategy-how you will achieve the goal
Tactic-what you will do to implement the strategy

Here's an example.

Goal: Generate $100,000 per month in interior painting sales.

Strategy: Be the Best Educator in the Industry, position us as the experts, and own the search results.

Tactic: Create a content library on your website answering every question anyone has ever asked about interior painting. Share these videos and articles with all incoming leads to build authority and trust. Share with influencers like Interior Designers, Home Inspectors, and others who stand in front of people who need interior painting done.

A quick note about the content library. Check out a couple books by my friend Marcus Sheridan. He's the author of

They Ask, You Answer, and *The Visual Sale*. Everything you need to know about creating great content that will position you as the industry leader and attract the right buyers to you is in those books.

When I create a marketing plan with my clients, I start with the goal. Then, we work together to create three main strategies. Finally, we figure out what three tactics they will take action on to execute each strategy. This takes time but is worth it.

Once your plan is done, execute it and track it. As you gather data, you can then make adjustments to the tactics.

Build Your Brand

Everything you do and don't do tells a story. Your company identity, the appearance of your people, how you answer the phone...or not. Everything either builds trust or strips it away.

What do people feel when they see your company? What contradictions are jumping out at them?

For example, you're a fence contractor. Someone searches online for "fence contractor near me" and comes across your website. They fill out a form and then.... crickets. It takes days instead of a few minutes for you to call them. Or you tell someone you will send them the proposal on Tuesday by 4pm. It's now Saturday, and they have to chase you down. Trust is quickly eroding, and now you're the typical contractor. Unorganized and chaotic.

This is one of the reasons why clients give contractors so much grief. They feel like they need to babysit you in order for you to do your part. This is one reason they tell you that you're too expensive and hire someone else. They don't trust you. You give them a Mercedes price and a Dollar General experience.

It's been said that good marketing is like a nice drive on a golf course. It puts the ball right next to the hole, setting you up for a 'gimme' putt (sales call). The stronger your brand the easier the sale.

It's on you to create an intentional story about your company. What do you want people saying about you when they talk to their friends? What do you want a past client to feel when they see your truck in the neighborhood?

You might do great work, but that's not enough. The things that surround the work matter more.

Play the Long Game

Another mistake that is made is having the wrong expectations when you market your business. Most think that the leads start flowing immediately after you turn on a marketing tactic. I hear things like, "I tried that video thing, and it didn't work." I ask how many videos they made, and the answer is always under five.

Market your business with patient urgency. Do what needs to be done NOW. Just know that it will take some time to grow. If you create a plan rooted in a strong strategy and the right tactics, it will work.

I've always approached marketing as not something that I do, but it's just who I am. Meaning, I am a marketer that happens to paint stuff, or build homes. I am my own biggest fan. I know that the more people who know about me the better the chances I have of selling my services. Marketing is an everyday thing, like waking up and taking a leak. This is not optional if you want to win the Contractor Fight. This is not optional if you want to change your financial situation.

The great news is that it's never been easier to market your business and build your brand. If you have a smartphone and a pulse, you can do it. If you are able to introduce yourself to another human and shake their hand...you can grow your business. It's an attitude. Quit making excuses and do it.

A Little Truth Bomb

Many contractors tell me they don't want to grow their business. They say they're happy with how it is or that they don't want the headaches of hiring more people. They bullshit me and tell me they can't get out of the field to do the 'owner' stuff.

This is all code for, "I don't trust myself."

They don't trust themselves to grow as a leader.

Fast forward a few years and they will be in the same place financially, maybe worse off. And their bodies will be a bit more beaten up. They will have worked their asses off and will have little to nothing to show for it.

It's your choice, of course. I choose to build a business, not just have a job working for a boss who can't get out of his own way.

Market your fucking business like a beast. Unapologetically build your brand. Be your own biggest fan. Get with the times and skate to where the puck is going...content, education, connection. Quit being stubborn and lazy and do what successful business owners do. If you love the field so much, go work for someone else. Otherwise, step up and run a real business.

I'll end this chapter with an article I wrote many years ago. It's one of my rants. It also gives you 10 tips to help you generate more leads and sales for your business.

Why I'm Pissed Off at Home Improvement Contractors

It's winter again, and I'm starting to see contractors freak out about not getting enough home improvement leads for their businesses.

I see this every year. Sadly, I see some of the same contractors posting the same crap they did a year ago on Facebook about how they need more business.

"My phone just stopped ringing. What are you guys doing to get more leads?"

"I don't know what to do. I don't have any work coming in and not sure how we're going to make it."

I'm a little pissed when I see posts like these because I told them so last year, last month and last week. I told them so 2 years ago and the year before that.

Each year contractors are surprised when the results are the same or worse than the year before.

Before you get all offended that I'd be pissed at a bunch of contractors for making the same stupid mistake every year, remember this: I'm one of them. As a contractor, I made just about every mistake you could make. It's from those experiences that I speak today. I'm not saying "I told you so" to rub your noses in it. I'm just calling it for what it is.

Let's move on to the meat of this article. The rest of this post is for the purpose of equipping the average home improvement contractor with what he needs to make sure this is the last year he has inconsistent lead flow.

Wait. One more rant.

Dear Contractor,

Get your head out of your ass. This is important stuff that will reduce your stress and bring in enough money to care for your loved ones. If you are content with being mediocre, then keep doing what you've been doing.

If you're ready to build a home improvement business that will serve you and make your life better, then keep reading.

Sincerely,

Tom

Marketing Tip 1: Marketing is Your Job

You've heard, "Work on your business, not in it." The biggest factor to your business being successful is how well you market it.

You may paint a beautiful house, lay carpet like a champ, or build a gorgeous water feature, but nobody will give a crap if they don't know you exist.

You need a marketing system that will produce qualified leads each day for your home improvement business. This will not happen by accident.

Your number 1 role in your company is to produce leads and sell work. Period. Without this, you have nothing.

Too many of you have been in business for 5, 10, 20 years, and you're still playing this "I don't have enough leads" game.

If you can't get this through your head, quit your business and get a job.

Marketing Tip 1b: There's No Magic Lead Tree

Stop counting on 3rd party lead sources like Angie's List, Houzz, Home Advisor, and the like.

Anyone that tells you that they are the Holy Grail of lead generation is full of shit.

You will get more leads when you commit to building your brand and working a marketing plan that is designed to attract your ideal clients.

Too many of you freak out when the phone stops ringing and then pay for a bunch of lame lead generation tactics. Don't spend a dime on any 3rd party savior until you create your marketing plan first.

Marketing Tip 2: Get Involved in Your Community

When someone hires a contractor, they are inviting them into their home. In my home, my people are precious to me. You are not getting in here if I don't trust you.

By getting involved in the community, you are giving people in your target area the opportunity to get to know you. When they know you and like you, they will eventually trust you unless you're a moron.

Trust leads to leads. Leads lead to sales.

Join your local chamber of commerce. Join a BNI group. Volunteer in a Rotary Club. Do an annual charity project.

Stop relying on the internet alone like it's some kind of 'easy' button.

Join a group and commit to it. Show up…clean, on time, and in the frame of mind that this is working on your business.

Andy Northey of R & A Water Features & Landscaping did over $500k from one group he belongs to. My old painting company did over $500k per year just from this as well.

Marketing Tip 3: Nuke Your Website

I have talked so much about this in the past. Most contractors have lousy websites. Your site should be all about the client and less about how awesome you think you are.

Speak to their pain. Make it easy for them to do business with you. Talk about pricing. Educate them and position yourself as the expert in your industry.

Pro Tip: Don't build your own site. You don't know what you're doing. You expect your clients to pay you top dollar for building stuff, right? Then, why do you go on the cheap with your website? Hire a pro and get out of their way.

Edit that's not in the original article: Looking to build an online sales machine that combines our Shin-Fu sales process with a website that attracts and converts your ideal clients? Check out https://contractorgrowthnetwork.com. Logan Shinholser and his team have mastered this.

Marketing Tip 4: Produce Content

"Don't drive traffic to the ghetto."

My good friend and marketer, Jason Thalman, said that to me years ago. Far too many contractors spend money on driving traffic to a shitty website and then wonder why no leads come through the site.

Create content that is relevant and valuable to your ideal clients. This, along with simple and clear design, will do more than paid traffic, back-linking strategies and any other flavor of the month your marketing guru sells you.

Without good content that meets needs, people will leave the site. Content will establish you as the expert. People trust and hire experts.

Grab your iPhone and shoot a video. Answer questions that people ask you…do project profiles.

Google will organically reward you.

Marketing Tip 5: Love Those Who Already Love You

I am amazed at how many home improvement contractors don't keep in touch with their past clients. **Moment of Truth:** I didn't either in my first 3 years of business. It cost me at least 2 million in revenue.

Your past clients already wrote you a check. That means they are very likely to do it again. If you don't stay in touch via an email marketing strategy, snail mail postcards, or phone calls...you are practically shoving them to your competitors.

Stop bitching about how clients leave you. Keep them warm with the content you create. Call them to let them know their warranty is up in 6 months and to have you out to fix anything.

Make the experience they have with you so awesome they'd cut a finger off before they left you.

I believe at least 80% of your leads should be from past clients and those they refer you to.

Marketing Tip 6: Learn to Up-Sell

Invest in sales training for your team. They will plant seeds that will be ready for harvest later (that means you'll have a lead later).

Contractors lose leads and sales because they don't have a system for selling additional work. Our Shin-Fu Sales Training will change this quickly.

Marketing Tip 7: Be Referral Worthy

Nobody will give a crap how awesome their project looks if the experience sucked.

I've polled many, many home improvement customers over the years and without fail, they have never once complained about the work you did. **They only complained about things like:**

- too long for you to call back & get out to their home

- too many days after you came to the house to get them a bid
- you won't return calls when there's a problem
- you suck at cleaning up

It's about the experience. If there were a Magic Lead Tree for you this would be it.

Marketing Tip 8: Pick a Lane and Stay There

Do you have a fancy name and expensive-looking brand identity and then go and offer a bunch of discounts?

Do you see what you're doing?

You're confusing the buyer. Are you high-end or cheap?

Position your business to connect with your ideal client. If you're a budget deck builder, then run that sale in the Money Mailer!

If you're the high-end remodeler in the town, steer clear from stuff like that.

How you position your business will affect your lead flow.

Marketing Tip 9: Build Your Team of Influencers

I did over $350k each year from what I call 'influencers.' These are the contractors that stand in front of my ideal clients each day.

Joe was a carpet guy who stood in front of hundreds of people each year schlepping his services. These clients of his would frequently ask if he knew a painter. This turned into work for me.

I also stood in front of people that needed Joe's carpet services every day.

I conservatively estimate that you can generate another 50 high-quality leads each year if you build your influencer network. How do you do that, you ask? Reach out to companies that you think would have a good fit with yours and set up a time to grab a beer or coffee. Give to them. They'll give to you. **This is a goldmine that, honestly, too many contractors are too lazy to tap into.**

Marketing Tip 10: Track Your Leads

If you don't track where your leads and sales come from you are pissing into the wind. Tracking allows you to make better decisions about where to spend your time and money in regard to marketing your business.

Identify the lead sources that add the most value to your business and optimize those. The things that don't get you results need to be dumped.

What kind of marketing plan do you have? Give your attention to creating a real marketing plan and you'll enjoy more leads and sales in the months and years to come.

Chapter 10: Quitters Never Win...Hmm

"Quitters never win and winners never quit."

I read that every day in the locker room at Wheaton North High School. I was fortunate to be part of a great football program run by an old Marine, Jim Rexilius. I am proud to be a Falcon.

Coach Rex inspired so many young men to get out of their comfort zones and achieve more. I can't imagine my life without the man. Often, he was the rock in my turbulent and stormy life. He was so impactful in my life that I was more afraid of letting him down than my own parents. I went to class and clawed my way to eligibility just so I didn't have to look him in the eyes and tell him I failed a class.

There was a word in the Falcon football program that was ingrained in every player. It was part of the culture there, the way we did things. You couldn't go 5 minutes without hearing a coach say it or the team chant it.

"Attack."

That's how we did things there. That was the tradition. That mindset was the foundation of a program that dominated the DuPage Valley Conference for years and earned a few state titles, including our commanding playoff run and lopsided championship win over Mount Carmel in 1986.

"Attack."
"Never quit."
"Sacrifice."
"Pay a price."
"Carry yourself with pride."

These phrases echoed throughout that program and brainwashed me...and, for the record, I believe that was a good thing.

This is probably why I was drawn to serve in the United States Marine Corps. Being part of a team that was rooted in the strong traditions of pride, honor, and commitment was attractive. Being part of *The Few and Proud* fired me up. Not everyone could do it. I loved being on a team like that.

After serving in the Marines, coaching High School Football for about 17 years, and coaching hundreds of business owners, I've learned a thing or two about the whole "Winners Never Quit" quote.

Sometimes you should quit.

"Tom! What happened to attack! Pay a price! Sacrifice!"

Sometimes you should quit.
As a contractor you work your ass off. If hard work and sacrifice were the only requirements for success, then a

career as a home improvement contractor would be the highest-earning career around.

You get up early.
Stay up late.
Set up the guys.
Run from meeting to meeting.
Throw on the tool belt and labor away for hours.
Meet potential clients.
Apologize for mistakes made by employees.
Type up estimates until after midnight.
Scramble to get a job done because one of your guys didn't show today and fucked the whole plan up.
Field calls from the unreasonable client who called you on Christmas morning.
Apologize to your spouse for having to miss dinner again...you just have to meet with this client.

Need I go on? I'm sure you can add another dozen things you do each week.

Sometimes you should quit. It may seem like I am encouraging you to quit at this point in the book. For some of you I am and think it would be a great idea to hang it up and go work for someone else.

Winning the Contractor Fight is like building a football program that has a tradition of kicking ass for a decade or more. The reason so many contractors struggle financially, go into debt, and don't have shit to show for their hard work and sacrifice after running a business for a couple decades is simple.

They like the *idea* of being a business owner, but they don't *do* the things successful business owners do.

Just like I've seen in the many football programs I've been a part of. Many young men like the idea of being on the team. Calling themselves a football player. Wearing the uniform. Running out on the field in front of the crowd. Getting a little recognition when there is some success. Mediocre programs are full of these guys. Those who liked the idea of being a football player, instead of guys who do what successful football players do.

The trades are full of mediocre owners who like the idea of driving around a badass truck that's all tatted up with their cool logo.

They like the idea of running out onto the field of play wearing their custom flat billed hat with their team colors on it. Don't forget the cool t-shirts they made up!

The mediocre owners blow off putting in the uncomfortable work of learning their numbers, learning how to market and sell. Learning how to lead and build a strong culture. This is like the football player who skips class, blows off the weight room, and eats like shit. He's a wannabe.

Here's a list of several things the #FW contractor does:

-creates a company budget
-gets sales training
-has regular team meetings
-creates clear job scopes
-job costs every job
-recruits for the team daily
-builds the brand daily
-owns his shit as a leader
-hires coaches
-invests in his team with training
-controls overhead

-hires people to implement profitable systems
-has tough conversations
-creates a clear career path for growth in the company
-embraces humility
-conducts weekly meetings
-tracks Key Performance Indicators (KPI's)
-learns to get out of the way

Are you wearing the uniform, or are you actually being a business owner?

If you continue to blow off the things those successful contractors do and are repeating the same year over and over... you know...busy, tired, unorganized, stale, more debt, the same or shrinking personal income, stress on the relationships, etc.... then, yes you should quit.

It will be better for your health, bank account, marriage, and your sanity.

Maybe you just haven't found your thing yet. Maybe you're happier working for someone else instead of carrying the load of running a business. That's totally ok. Nobody is shaming anyone here.

If we're not willing to do the things it takes to be successful at something, then why do it?

You can still 'attack.' Just not in this endeavor. Find something else that wakes you up and inspires you to do what's required.

This is where I'm supposed to say shit like, "find something you love, and you'll never work a day in your life." Many will tell you that when you're passionate about something you will automatically do what's required.

That's bullshit. We all drag our feet from time to time.

I will tell you this. If you really want to own and run a successful business, then do the damn work. Nobody cares about your feelings. Are you going to do your job as the owner or not? Success comes from taking steps each day, learning from the mistakes and being better the next day.
Many of you reading this are taking steps and making mistakes, but not learning and growing from them. You're in the same place you were a year or two or three ago.

How have you grown in the past couple of years? Not just topline company revenue...that's easy.

I'm talking about as a leader. Your happiness and contentment. Stress levels. Your health and relationships. Your profit and personal income. You get the idea.

Success and failure both leave clues. What evidence are you leaving behind that would support you staying the course and not quitting?

What evidence is there in your life that owning a contracting business is a good thing? Is your life better off for it?

Sometimes you need to quit and find something else to win at. Win at something in another industry. Win as a right-hand employee for another contractor. Find a way to win instead of getting your ass handed to you year after year.

Some have told me to just believe in myself and success will come. Eh...

How about making a commitment and checking the damn boxes each day that are required of you? No more procrastinating the important things. No more pointing the finger at the economy, who lives in the White House or the unlicensed guys in your area for your lack of success.

Are you going to do what fucking winners do or are you just content wearing the uniform and calling yourself a business owner?

Whatever you choose, go all in.

Tom Reber

Chapter 11: The Profit Path

I will call him "Sam."

He called me up looking for help because he had lost money three years in a row in his flooring business. He shared a few things with me about how he was pricing his work to make better than a 50% gross profit, cut the fat from his overhead and had a strong closing rate on the leads that came in.

At one point he said to me, "we just need to do a better job of making our clients happy." The funny thing about that statement was that they excelled in getting great reviews and their referrals were strong and frequent.

Sam, like many contractors, went straight to "I need to make my clients happy" when he was faced with a financial ass kicking. In fact, most contractors go there or to the quality of their work when profits are low. It's natural to think if I'm not making money, I need to do better work and make the clients happy and that will fix the money leaks.

In this chapter, I want to introduce you to The Profit Path. This concept has helped numerous contractors right the ship and make consistent and intentional profit.

"Intentional profit?"

My second year of business I had about $50,000 left in my business bank account. The problem was that it was an accident, I had no idea how I pulled that off. Knowing why we make or lose money is important. The goal of a business is to make a profit. Some of you would say that having $50,000 in the bank was a nice accident! But, I want to build the type of companies that set a profit goal and reach it on purpose, year after year. Maybe I should call this Profit on Purpose instead?

Intentional profit is the result of the right things being done in the right order. For fun, I have randomly placed the steps to profit below. Take a guess what the correct order is.

HINT: Profit is the last one.

- Quality Work
- Employee Satisfaction
- Leadership
- Client Loyalty
- Profit
- Employee Loyalty
- Client Satisfaction
- Employee Productivity
- Culture

I'll address them in the correct order for you. How did you do? I've done this exercise for years in workshops and with coaching clients, and nobody has nailed it the first time. Let's dig into why the order needs to be what it is.

Leadership

Everything starts at the top. Your job as a leader is to positively influence your team. It's to create a vision of what could be in the future and guide the people there. You're an escort to the promised land.

Sadly, most of us suck at leading until we make a choice to be a student of it. I once threatened to throw an employee out a window if he didn't stain something the way I wanted. I yelled at people, gave them shit for every little thing, and expected them to read my mind and pretty much train themselves.

I didn't throw him out the window.

Strong leadership is the most important step on this path. A strong leader sets a clear target, guides his people, makes them feel safe and supported, and earns their trust.

Think about yourself for a moment. How do you show up for your people? Chaotic, scatter-brained, directionless, and winging everything, lacking consistency? That was me for a long time. Most contractors struggle with this because they have never been taught what it really means to lead.

Imagine how strong you'd be as a leader if you put in half the time you put in learning your trade into your development as a leader?

One tip... practice Patient Urgency as a leader. When you spot an area you need to grow in, attack it. Then, be patient with yourself because it's going to take time to grow and make positive changes.

Failing to commit to this first step on the Profit Path is like putting two finish coats of paint on a surface and then a top coat of primer.

Culture

Culture is how we do things here. It's the intersection of what we expect and what we tolerate. Strong leaders create a strong and intentional culture.

"My guys don't _____."

Fill in the blank.

Show up on time.
Fill out their timecards.
Finish jobs at or under the budgeted hours.

If you expect them to show up on time and let them slide when they don't, you're creating a culture of 'anything goes.'

Jobs not finishing on time consistently? Same thing. Anything goes.

The culture you have is the culture you are tolerating. You have created it.

The way we do things here.

Let's jump into the home for a minute. You tell your teenage son to clean his room, or he can't go out with his friends. Yet, when he doesn't clean the room, you cave and let him go when he promises to clean it later. This is how we do things here. An expectation is set and then, whatever happens, happens.

"Tom, if I enforce things with my team, I might lose them. I can't afford to lose people because it's so hard to find good employees." I hear that all the time and I understand. However, so much stress we feel as business owners is self-imposed. How do we build the culture we want without being a dick?

What do you want? That's the first question. Define what the ideal culture looks like to you. Here are a few ways to start to figure this out.

Finish this sentence: This is the type of place where we...

Answer these:

What do you hope never changes about your current culture?
What do you want to change immediately?
When an employee talks about his work at a family BBQ on Sunday, what do you want him to say?
When a client is telling her friend about her experience with you, what would it sound like?

These will set you on the path to clarity.

A few other very important things...

1. Not tolerating certain things does not mean you're a jerk or have to be a hard ass. Building the culture you want takes more carrot than stick.
2. Creating a strong culture will require you to train your people. It will require patience and a commitment to playing the long game.

3. Consistency is your friend. If you say you will have a weekly meeting at 7am on Wednesdays and all your people need to be there, have the meeting. Start on time. Finish on time.

You already have a culture in your company. Write down 3-5 words to describe it now. Are you getting what you want?

Employee Satisfaction

You might be noticing that The Profit Path is an inside-out game. Take care of me first. Intentionally build a culture I want and then move to my employees.

Most think we need to take care of our customers first. Nope. Get oxygen. Meaning, take care of you and your own peeps, then you're ready to serve at greater levels.

Employee satisfaction is not just the money. Yes, money is important. In fact, pay them more than anyone in your area so it's not an issue. Just make sure the type of culture you create expects big boy results for the big boy money.

Ask your people about their goals at work and in their personal lives. Help them get what they want, and you will get what you want.

According to Merriam-Webster, the definition of the word 'satisfied' means "pleased or content with what has been experienced or received.'

What is their experience with you as a leader? With the culture? Are they respected? Are they satisfied with the growth opportunities you are providing? Are they recognized for the good stuff or just called out for the mistakes? Are they on edge due to the chaotic culture you have allowed or are they secure in their future with you?

It's easy to blow off our people and put our focus on the 'work.' Just remember, this is the right work in the long run. Committing to satisfying your employees doesn't mean you are a pushover and give them everything they want and allow them to run the show. It means providing a place where they can write their own future with you because of the clarity, structure and opportunities you provide.

Employee Loyalty

Many experience high employee or subcontractor turnover because they drop the ball in the satisfaction department.

A satisfied employee is a loyal one.

Several times a year my employees would be tapped on the shoulder and offered more money at other companies. We had amazing people and our competitors knew it. They never left. They were "pleased or content with what has been experienced or received' in my company.

During the Great Recession in 2008, we had to reduce costs and that included all employees taking a 20% pay cut. My partner and I took 30% cuts. This decision made it harder on our people to make ends meet at home. We knew it would hurt, but we also knew it had to be done for a period of time. I told the team that I understood if they needed to leave. I told them to do what they needed to support their families.

I also told them I believed we were stronger together than apart.

Not one employee left. They were loyal to each other and to us because they were "pleased or content with what has been experienced or received." Satisfaction matters.

Employee Productivity

Satisfied employees are loyal. A satisfied and loyal employee is more productive. They look forward to coming to work and being part of a strong culture. They don't dread Mondays.

This attitude of happiness and contentment sends a message and helps build your brand. I remember getting a call once from a dude who lived across the street from a house we were painting. He shared with our Office Manager that he had watched our teamwork for several days (he was retired) and was blown away by the smiles, the cleanliness, and the amount of work they produced in a day!

He hired us to paint his house.

Production and profits increase when you take care of your people first.

Quality Work

High-quality work is an expectation. Clients expect a company to consistently perform the thing they do at a high level. I've heard many contractors say they wish their teams were more consistent in their quality and production. One job they knock it out of the park. The next, they lay a turd and make the most ridiculous and remedial mistakes.

They say happy people do better work. I agree. I've lived it and I've seen it. When I'm happy and content I always approach my work with more pride and optimism. I've seen it in the teams I've led and worked on over the years.

Following The Profit Path and looking at things in the right order will improve your consistency. When quality drops go back to the start and put your eyes on you as the leader and ask yourself "What does the team need from me to improve the issues?"

Client Satisfaction

"My work should speak for itself."
"I did a great job installing that tile. I don't know why they didn't give me a better review."
"We are the best painting company in the city. I can't believe they didn't hire us. Cheap assholes."

Doing great work (high quality) is the bare-bones minimum expectation of a client. Think about when you go to a nice restaurant and order your food. You expect it's going to be high quality. I'm never surprised when I eat my dinner and the food is good!

"Damn. No way! I can't believe this steak is so good.!"

However, the one thing that can ruin that steak is the experience. Everything surrounding the food. My Queen and I once enjoyed some great food at a high-end restaurant outside of Chicago. She said, "This food is amazing. Too bad it comes with this shitty waitress."

The same goes for your work. We painted hundreds of homes a year in one of my companies. The actual paint job was rarely the thing people loved the most about working with us. Again, people expected high quality when they hired a professional painting company.

It was everything that surrounded the paint job that would make or break us.

How we answered the phones.
How we communicated and set expectations.
How our people looked, talked and acted.
Did we leave a mess?
Did we do what we said we would do when we said we would do it?
Was it easy for people to work with us?
Did we Mind the Gap? That means were they communicated within the time between when they hired us and when we started the job? This is when most contractors go silent, and the client is wondering what happens next. Without clear and consistent communication, they will make up their own stories.

If you want satisfied clients pay close attention to the things that surround the actual work you do.

This is an unfair advantage that will put and keep you at the top.

Client Loyalty

Put yourself in a client's shoes for a moment. Imagine that the contractor you hired did great work, but they left a mess. Or they were a bit of a pain in the ass to communicate with and you felt you were always chasing them to find out what was happening.

The work was great, but the experience wasn't. This alienates them instead of creating loyalty. I sold hundreds of jobs in my career because the last company they hired "did great work, but they were a pain to deal with."

When you follow The Profit Path you will eventually create a loyal client that can't imagine ever hiring or referring anyone but you.

Profit

This is the pot of gold we are all pursuing. Consistent and intentional profit. Financial profit and brand profit.

Strong leadership creates a strong culture, which satisfies employees. A satisfied employee is loyal and happy and will perform higher quality work. This high-quality work is the first brick in the client satisfaction wall. Creating a great experience finishes the wall and earns loyalty. This loyalty makes your life easier because you're building a good name and brand which produces consistent profits.

I can't stress enough the importance of being consistent as a leader. This requires personal discipline to stay the course when you're tempted to stray from the plan. Plan your weeks and days to support your journey down The Profit Path and follow through on what you plan. Spend your time on the high-impact activities that will guide your team and build the culture you envision.

Tom Reber

Chapter 12: The People Game

Human beings are all the same. In fact, we all have pretty much the same fears and the same needs. The People Game is about helping you to understand these fears and what you can do as a leader to reduce those fears and meet the needs these fears create. This applies to your employees as well as your clients. The most common fears are:

Death
The Outsider
An Unclear Future
Chaos
Insignificance

Death

At some level, all humans fear death. The thought of not waking up one day can be sobering. There's also financial and relational death. Things die and it kind of freaks us out a bit. This fear of death creates a need for security. As a leader, we have a responsibility to provide security to those we employ.

Want to win your people over? Then, do your part and invest in the training and equipment that will prove to them you care about their well-being. One of the greatest gifts we can give people is security. If your top guy comes to work tomorrow with seven fingers, make sure he goes home with the same seven.

Many years ago, I acquired an amazing employee for my team. He came from one of my competitors. I asked him why he wanted to join our team and his reply always stuck with me.

"I'm tired of how the boss takes shortcuts and makes us do things that are not safe. He won't rent a lift or purchase harnesses."

He went on to share examples of how his old employer thought investing in being safe was too expensive and how he had left a fellow employee high and dry when he fell and got hurt.

Many contractors make it harder on themselves to build their teams because they don't show their people that they truly care about them and their safety.

The Outsider

Have you ever hired a new guy for the crew, and nobody liked him? I have.

"I don't like his attitude."
"I'm not sure he's going to get along with the other guys."
"His work isn't that good."

"He's slow. We don't need him."

These are some things I would hear when we brought a new guy onto the team. I have coached hundreds of contractors and pretty much 100% of the time when we get to this topic they all can relate: Nobody likes the new guy.

People fear the outsider. We wonder if they're going to take our spot. Will they be better than me? Will they screw up the 'mojo' of the crew?

Think about the clients you serve. Your company is an outsider. You're new to them unless it's a repeat customer. And, even then you still may be.

We show up, bang on the door and invade their life. Often, we are big guys who are tatted up and a bit loud. It can be intimidating for people who don't really know us. The Outsider.

In both cases, with our own employees and with our clients, there are many unknowns for them. It's our responsibility to build community and connection. It's our job to foster a positive connection and build relationships that ease this fear.

With your team, building community could look like:

-weekly lunch with the team
-company breakfast on the first day a new person starts
-celebrating major life events or birthdays
-going on a quarterly hike or playing paintball
-recognizing them for the good they do at the weekly company meeting

The more you can foster relationships in your company the stronger your team will be. The more you can show them you care about them and are here to support them in their success, the stronger the team will be. The little things matter.

Reducing the fear of the outsider with clients can include things like:

-sending links to your team bios on your website so they can see who will be coming to their home
-short video introductions of your foremen
-weekly updates on schedule prior to starting their project
-content on your website that is relevant to all the questions and concerns they have

It's been said that people do business with those they know, like, and trust. I believe a stronger community is built with our teams and clients when the same happens.

An Unclear Future

People want to know what's coming next. I once coached a multi-million-dollar painting company that was highly profitable and growing. During a few conversations with some key employees, I got word that several of the people were looking for other jobs. As I spoke with these employees, they voiced concerns that the company was struggling and was running out of work. So, they went looking for gainful employment elsewhere.

I asked the owner how the workload was looking, and he said they were booked out for months and sales were better than ever.

Two futures were being told to me. One of a struggling company and little work. The other of record sales and months of a backlog for the teams.

After sharing my dilemma with the boss man, it came to light that the company had recently changed how it communicated to the teams about upcoming work. This change resulted in the teams not knowing what projects were on the radar and the result...they started making up their own stories.

Scott was a landscaper in the Midwest. He had been in business for over fifteen years, had a great reputation and always had plenty of work. But, this year, the year I worked with him, he said they had an increasing rate of people canceling work after it was sold. Due to high demand and a shrinking labor force in the trades, his projects were often scheduled out farther than normal and people didn't want to wait.

I get that. Waiting sucks. But waiting sucks more when you're in the dark.

The fear of an unclear future drives the need for clarity. Real clarity prevents many problems.

Back to Scott and his clients pulling the ejection lever and bailing out for other contractors. The root of this issue was silence. He would sell a job, get a deposit and schedule it. He would pre-plan the job and have a clear scope of work for the team. He would work behind the scenes to ensure everything was organized and ready to go so his company could deliver on another great project. Often, he would spend weeks preparing for a job. The biggest problem with all of that was that his clients had no idea. They never heard from Scott after the sale and started making up their own stories.

Silence separates.

In both stories above an unclear future was hijacking the success of the companies.

What was the fix?

Clarity.

My painter friend went back to clear and visible communication for the crew's upcoming production schedule. He put a monitor in the shop that showed the calendar. Whenever the employees came into the shop they would glance up and see a full calendar. They'd see new jobs added each day and knew what was happening tomorrow, next week and next month. The result? Nobody jumped ship and he went on to several more record years of sales.

Clarity.

Scott began to Mind the Gap. This is a process I teach that fills the time between the sale and the start date of the project with clear and relevant communication. It includes sending weekly updates about the company schedule and the project to the client. This can be done with video, phone calls, texts or emails.

Simply sending a link to a piece of content about "How to get your home ready for your project" or "meet your Foreman" or "what we're working on this week to get ready for your project" can go a long way in minding the gap. Most contractors go dark during this gap and this causes the clients to make up their own stories like "they forgot about me. I better hire someone else." When you Mind the Gap the client has a better experience, sees more value in you, buyer's remorse decreases, and trust is built.

Silence separates. In all of your relationships, do your part to provide a clear future.

"But, Tom. I don't know what is going to happen each day. I don't have a fucking crystal ball!"

That's an excuse for not making a plan and communicating the plan. We all know things change...Mother Nature gets pissed and screws up your schedule or suppliers run behind. Shit happens.

Just communicate it and you'll be miles ahead of every other contractor in your area.

Chaos

Where does chaos keep showing up in your business?

Not sure. Ask your team and your clients.

For years I would bid and sell jobs to make a 50% or better gross profit and then wonder on the back end of the job why we didn't make the target profit.

The culprit was chaos instead of order. I gave no clear scopes of work, didn't have pre-planning meetings and had no training whatsoever for my people. The result was a chaotic environment that stressed everyone out and a small bank account.

Clients were upset. Employees were annoyed. Most of my time was spent being a firefighter. The remaining time, a professional Apologizer.

When I coach people or speak to groups, chaos is the most common complaint I hear. It's truly the low-hanging fruit that will help them immediately have a stronger business. Eliminate the self-imposed chaos and replace it with some order...bam! Huge changes immediately.

"Complete disorder and confusion." That's the definition of chaos.

Employees are confused and don't know what you want from them. They don't have any idea whether or not they are doing a good job...or even what needs to happen in order to do a good job for you. Clients are confused because they thought _____. Fill in the blank.

Getting clarity will often eliminate chaos. An unclear future and chaos are siblings. As are clarity and order.

I see so many contractors trying to build their teams only to be let down again and again. "I can't keep anyone. I pay well and give them a truck and they jump ship for a buck an hour."

Most people leave because their boss sucks, not because of money. The boss has built a culture of insecurity, an unclear future and chaos.

Most clients are unhappy with a company for the same reasons.

Insignificance

Oxford Languages defines insignificance as "too small or unimportant to be worth consideration."

Want to be an expert in the people game? Make people feel important. Our fear of being insignificant drives the need for importance. As one of my business partners, Derek Johnson, frequently shares, everyone is wearing an imaginary sign around their neck that says, "Make me feel important."

Imagine how things would change if we just did that?

Clients and employees would feel like they were heard, understood and respected.

How do we make people feel important? Ask them.

"Mary, what would need to happen on your project in order for you to feel important to us?"
"Joe, what would it look like for you to feel important here at Tom's Construction?"

Start by asking.

Here are a few tips for making your clients feel important:

-Mind the Gap
-Answer the Phone
-Do what you said you'd do when you said you'd do it
-Communicate and tell the truth
-Respect their time, their people, their property and their money

Here are a few for making your employees feel important:

-Get their input on problems
-Treat them like adults
-Recognize them when they do something good
-Invest in them/Regular training
-Be patient when mistakes are made
We could list things for days that would make someone else feel important. Remember earlier in the book we talked about The Profit Path? This stuff answers the "how do I satisfy my employees and customers?" question.

Continually work on you as a leader. Grow in your understanding of people and you will have massive influence both in and outside of your company.

Chapter 13: Non-Negotiable Values

I call them NNV's. Non-negotiable values.

A value is something you hold as extremely important. I can't stress enough how crucial identifying your values are to your success.

Your values will guide you. They help you make decisions. They protect your personal integrity. They will help you to choose good partners.

They also raise morale and production. They empower your employees. They improve employee and client retention.

Many business owners struggle to hire properly. You run a job ad, and someone responds. You're impressed with their experience, and they tell you how amazing they are over the course of a couple interviews. You make the offer, and they accept. You're happy. They're happy. Things are going great until a few months down the road you start having issues with them.

Yes, they have the skills you need, but you're not aligned on other things, and they end up quitting or you fire them. You've heard "hire for character and teach the skill." Yes, character is huge. But, how do you define it? How do you know their 'character' is the right one? Your NNV's map it out for you.

Your values are the rebar of your foundation. They provide a blueprint for all to follow. They provide the specs on how you will build your team. Don't blow this off.

In The Contractor Fight, these are the NNV's I established. It's important to note that these are MY VALUES. My team may come and go. Clients will come and go. I counsel owners to create values that are deeply connected to who they are.

The Contractor Fight Values

Own Your Crap
Positive Peeps Only
Get Oxygen
Roll the Red
Play the Long Game
Shed Assumptions
Go For It
Earn Confidence
Simplify

Before I explain these in a little more detail, I want to share the two main ways we keep them front and center in my companies. First, we open meetings sharing how we lived out one of our NNV's in the past week. This is just a little nudge to keep them on our radar. Second, when we need to make a big decision or choose who to partner with or hire for our team, we run all that through our values to make sure we align on most of them. These NNV's go with me wherever I go. Regardless of the company I run or what I do, these tag along and apply to anything I do.

Own Your Crap- this is where it starts with me. If we don't have self-awareness, we will limit our growth. Take responsibility for your performance. No throwing others under the bus or playing the victim card. Want to get better? It starts with you.

Positive Peeps Only- life and business are challenging enough. I don't want or need pessimistic people on my team. We can have a bad moment or a shitty day, but overall, the cup needs to be half-full if you're going to fit in here.

Get Oxygen- we get ours first. Be selfish when it comes to taking care of you and yours. Pay yourself first. Take care of your mind and body. Make sure you do what you need to strengthen your relationships at home.

Roll the Red- be excellent in whatever we do. Always strive to improve the experiences we give each other and our clients.

Play the Long Game- do what's right ten years from now. No shortcuts. We are not about one transaction but adding value for the long-term.

Shed Assumptions- don't be a mind-reader. We don't give advice or criticize without first understanding the context of someone's situation or point of view. Ask questions and listen with curiosity.

Go For It- take the shot. If it's ethical, safe and you feel it's best for the relationship or the company...do it. You're trusted.

Earn Confidence- we have a responsibility to show up every day and earn the trust of each other, our clients and our industry partners. We can't expect to win today because we did yesterday.

Simplify- keep things simple at all costs. Complicated creates chaos. Always look to get to the simplest level of any problem and offer the simplest solution.

I can't express how helpful this is when your whole team is on the same page. Instead of being in a boat and rowing in different directions, you will all be focused at the root level in your organization, which will produce huge results down the road.

Chapter 14: Random Thoughts About Random Stuff

The following are just a few things that flow through my head on a regular basis. Some come in the form of encouragement. Some were spoken to me in an attempt to kick me in the ass. Maybe something here will inspire you or give you some perspective.

- "Tom. You need to stop being the weak link here." This was said to me by my Queen, Lee. I was being an idiot. She called me out. This has stuck with me, and I reflect on this often to make sure I am never the weak link again.
- 90% of your thoughts are negative. Be picky about what you allow into your brain. Be intentional in what you say to yourself.
- Whatever gets your focus and attention will grow. Good or bad.
- Increase your confidence!

- o Take care of your machine (body).
- o Make sure you hang with those who make you better.
- o Overdose on discomfort. That's where you grow and prove you have what it takes.
- o Keep the promises you make to yourself.
- "What does my future require of me now, in this moment?"
- Your thoughts drive your beliefs. You will act in accordance with what you believe. Your results come from your actions. Be careful what you put into your brain. You truly become what you tell yourself. You truly get what you focus on.
- Your habits are a preview of your future.
- You only have so many fucks to give each day. Don't waste your energy on things that don't matter.

Do

Success is wanted by all but achieved by few. There are levels of success that are attained, but rarely the level that most envision for themselves.

Why is that? Why do so many have such big goals yet fail to come even close to getting there?

My definition of success…

"Whatever you want from life…or a relationship…or a business."
If you achieve what you really want…you're a success.

We're talking about YOUR success.

What do you really want? What do you want your life to look like? Time? Money? Relationships? Health?

Stop looking around at everyone else. What matters to you? What do you want?

This is where many will start saying things like, "I would be happy with just…"

Fill in the blank: _____

Enough money to pay my bills
A good work-life balance

Sorry. Not specific enough. Nor, in my opinion, bold enough. Seriously, you only want 'enough to pay your bills?'

Nope. Not good enough. This is where I will call BS on your personal definition of success.

I'm here to challenge your view of yourself and what you're capable of.

I believe you can live a life where you never worry about money again. A life where you have a hot and steamy relationship with your person. A life where you call the shots as to how you spend your time. A life where you're nobody's little bitch.

How's that sound?

How to Get There

Asking 'how' is premature.

First… what do you want. Then, get clear on why it matters.

The how is easier when these two equations are answered with absolute clarity.

So, what do you really want? This is where most fail. They don't take the time to get honest about this and instead chase someone else's definition of success. After you define 'what' nail the 'why.'

What is your target?
Why is your fuel?
What clarity sounds like...

"I want to work 3 days per week on my business and earn $250k per year. This will allow me to be in my kids' lives to the degree that I want and coach football so I can have an impact in the lives of young men."

"I want to build a business that can operate without me for 3 months at a time so I can travel with my wife and see the world with her."

"I want to earn $350k per year so I can fund the retirement years of my parents who don't have enough savings and have health issues."

Don't undersell your potential.

After you're clear on what you want, make the commitment. Clarity and commitment come before the "how."

Here's the 'how.'

Do the work it takes to move closer to those targets. Each day. No wasted movement. No wasted opportunities.

Reverse engineer what it will take and then map out your actions each day, week and month to move closer. This creates momentum and will compound over time.

You want to make $350k? What's that come down to weekly? What will be required of you to get there? How many jobs will you need to perform? How many leads are needed? What profit margin do you need in order to put $350k in your pocket? Math is unemotional and tells the truth.

Most know what they need to do. Unfortunately, they're waiting to take action. They think there's a hack coming their way. They listen to more podcasts. Watch more YouTube videos. Read more articles. Ask the same questions in industry Facebook Groups. They do this in hopes of finding the fast track.

Instead. DO. Do what you've already learned. Do what you already know you're procrastinating. You know you need to raise prices. DO. You know your marketing needs a rehab. DO. You know you need to fire the toxic dickface who works for you. DO.

I've helped thousands of contractors over the years. The biggest difference between the winners and losers is implementation.

Derek went from 60k a year to over 400k in personal income in about three years. Why? Because I told him to price his landscaping work at 50% gross profit. He actually thought I said 60% and did that instead. That was one of the many things he DID. In fact, he DOES so much that his nickname is The Implementer.

James paid off 80k in debt in six months....and just under $200k in a year. He also more than quadrupled his personal income in those six months. Why? We taught him to pre-qualify his leads on the phone and protect his time. And he DID it. We also told him to price his work at 50% gross profit. Unlike most GC's who normally argue that they can't do that as a GC...James DID it.

For every Derek and James I tell you about, I could share 100 that didn't DO. They kept looking for ways to be an exception instead of doing what they were taught.

I wish I had something sexier for you here. But I don't. For those that like simple lists here's this. My promise is if you check these boxes, you'll be on your way to your success.

-Be your own biggest fan. Market your business daily. Invest in it. Time and money. Be a Hunter & a Farmer.
-Learn to sell. Most don't know how. They just run their mouths. This takes consistent practice.
-If something costs you $1, charge your customer at last $2.
-Help others succeed. Stop being a scarcity-minded leader.

Making money is easy. Your income reveals your mindset and your intention to implement.

Acknowledgments

The first time I held him he crapped his pants. Dakota was one day old when he joined our family as our firstborn. He has grown up to be a man who speaks his truth. You never wonder where he stands on things, and it is one of many things I respect about him. He's also a man who loves and cares deeply for people. He's a protector, a shoulder to lean on and passionately loyal. He currently serves our amazing country as a United States Marine.

I remember the first time I saw her. She was 9 months old and dressed in traditional Chinese baby clothes. When my eyes locked onto hers, I was forever changed. My daughter Iris is the epitome of beauty. She's full of life, energy and compassion. She is a strong young woman. I love her curiosity, entrepreneurial spirit and kindness. She's doing life right now as a High School student with big dreams for her future.

"Because my son is there." That was my answer when someone asked why I was going to Haiti to adopt my son Tiga. Sometimes you just know when something is right, and this was one of those times. Tiga is Mr. Steady. He's a peacemaker, comedian and dreamer. His smile & charm will

127

take him far. His love for people will take him farther. Today, he's finding his way as he works in the HVAC industry.

Dakota, Tiga, Iris,
Thank you for your patience & love. I am a better man because of the three of you.

Maddie & Noel- the two of you are newer to my life as a result of the amazing relationship I have with your mother. You are strong, beautiful and talented. I love you both and am grateful that you are in my life. I look forward to creating many memories together as we all walk through this life we've been blessed with.

About the Author

Tom Reber is an entrepreneur, business coach, podcaster, founder of The Contractor Fight & Battleground Programand HGTV Host. His content has helped hundreds of thousands of home improvement contractors improve their lives and businesses.

Tom Reber

Tom coaches and advises business owners and CEOs on how to lead better, build stronger teams and scale their businesses profitably.

Tom is a United States Marine Corps veteran, lover of fine tequila and Kettlebell fanatic. He is originally from Wheaton, IL, and now resides in Colorado.